Ghosts of Southeastern Minnesota

Schiffer Publishing Ltd.

4880 Lower Valley Road, Atglen, Pennsylvania 19310

D1213817

Designed by Stephanie Daugherty
Type set in Still Time/NewBskvll BT

ISBN: 978-0-7643-3054-4

Printed in China

Schiffer Books are available at special discounts for bulk purchases for sales promotions or premiums. Special editions, including personalized covers, corporate imprints, and excerpts can be created in large quantities for special needs. For more information contact the publisher:

Schiffer Publishing Ltd.
4880 Lower Valley Road
Atglen, PA 19310
Phone: (610) 593-1777
Fax: (610) 593-2002
E-mail: Info@schifferbooks.com

Please visit our web site catalog at
www.schifferbooks.com

We are always looking for people to write books on new and related subjects. If you have an idea for a book, please contact us at the above address.

This book may be purchased from the publisher. Include $5.00 for shipping. Please try your bookstore first. You may write for a free catalog.

In Europe, Schiffer books are distributed by:
Bushwood Books
6 Marksbury Ave.
Kew Gardens
Surrey TW9 4JF,
England
Phone: 44 (0)208 392-8585
Fax: 44 (0)208 392-9876
E-mail: Info@bushwoodbooks.co.uk

Website: www.bushwoodbooks.co.uk

Free postage in the UK. Europe: air mail at cost. Try your bookstore first.

Dedication

To those who explore the unknown, and to things that go bump in the night.

Acknowledgements

I 'd like to acknowledge those who have contributed to the writing of this book, specifically to all of the individuals through emails, internet, phone, and personal visits who I interviewed. Thanks for taking the time to tell me you stories, no matter how difficult and frightening they were.

I'd also like to thank Lisa and Michelle and the rest at Twin Cities Paranormal Society (TCPS) for allowing me to come along on their investigation in Mantorville. Thanks also to Melisa for setting things up in Mantorville.

A special thanks to my editor, Dinah Roseberry, at Schiffer Publishing for giving me the chance to write such a fun and exciting book!

Lastly, kudos go to my wife, Nancy, and my two boys, Zach and Alex. The words I write come from the heart, which is where they are always.

Foreword

*D*o you believe in ghosts? Do you find yourself wondering from time to time about the supernatural? Have you had paranormal experiences occur in your life, or know those around you who have? Claiming that you believe in ghosts to friends and family can raise many eyebrows, or create a few chuckles as they toss you off as some ghost-busting freak. Which only makes you wonder yourself. You become confused and ask yourself, did it really happen? Even if you have not had an experience, you question why you believe in ghosts, why you think the paranormal is real.

Like it or not, some of us have been chosen by the quietly drifting spirits among us, to carry the ghoulish baton, leading them in the battle of belief. It seems that some ghosts are screaming for attention, bellowing out fitful shrieks and making playful recordings, or calling out desperately for help. But are they the ones asking for help, or is it us? Is there some energy force within us that is making the ghost appear? What are ghosts and where do they come from?

I'm sure some of you reading this book are hardcore aficionados on the ghostly subject, trudging through ectoplasm on dark, moonlit nights just around midnight. Or staying up all night in a proposed haunted house, recording and interviewing the living—and the dead. My hats off to you—it takes great courage to overcome the fear of the unknown.

Your bravery in the paranormal battlefields is not far from other early explorers, other adventurers such as Lewis and Clark, Christopher Columbus, or Marco Polo. Exploring and mapping out the unknown is riveted with exciting possibilities, igniting the fire of what makes life, while stabbing at the thoughts of death and the afterlife.

Where do we go once we are dead? The scientist within you must know, must succeed, recording and observing the strange activity around you. Of course, in the paranormal world, the science itself is unknown, making the journey that much more difficult—and dangerous. This brave adventure devoid of all logic and reason only adds to the terrifying supernatural awareness that surrounds you while sitting in the dark, waiting for the spirits to communicate with you.

Others reading this book may be encamped with a different point of view. They are 'on the fence' with ghosts, their belief teetering between what their perception is and what they have experienced. The mind plays an interesting game with what it has experienced, working diligently at making sure everything can be explained. Many supernatural events for the 'wanna believe in ghosts' group are ignored, with the mind not wanting to know about such things, not wanting to deal with the issue. Other unusual events are initially recognized, but then rationalized by presumed common logic and reason. Some in the 'wanna believe in ghosts' group switch to the dark side, where they conclude that there are no such things as ghosts. Others switch to the ghostly side, where their beliefs in the supernatural become deeply entrenched. Still, many remain on the fence, until they pass on to the afterlife. Then they'll know. But will it be too late?

Of course, moving onto the afterlife will provide the final answer to the truth about ghosts (or no truth at all, depending on your belief). But coming back to our world after you die has proven to be a difficult task. The great magician Houdini had tried, vowing to return from his death and prove to all that the afterlife is real. Can the trip be made back to this life? Perhaps that's something you'll discover while reading this book. It is up to us to attempt as best we can a way in which to shed light on the supernatural truth, perhaps altering the concept from supernatural to just natural. Ghost hunting and ghost stories provide a means of transforming our concept of what is natural. The stories provide a basis in which the hunting can begin. The hunting of the haunted tries to capture the ghost, recording it by various methods, and providing proof that the spirits are there.

Is this book for you? I can't answer that (of course you can buy it and find out!). If you're a ghost-hunting junkie, I hope you will find this book entertaining and perhaps a little enlightening. If you are a techno-geek looking for solid evidence that ghosts exist, I'm afraid you'll have to look further (and let me know what you find out!). This book is filled with numerous true ghost stories, along with the history behind the actual paranormal events. It also has a few novice ghost hunting expeditions that I took, with some surprising results. Surprising myself especially, as I am one of those 'on the fence', more a skeptic of ghosts than anything. I've had supernatural experiences in my life, but nothing extreme.

I'm hoping you'll come along with me on this journey into the true ghost stories of Southeastern Minnesota. I may not be a seasoned veteran ghost hunter, but I don't think you need to be. If the ghosts are there, and they want to talk to you, they will. The more experienced paranormal investigators will likely find more evidence faster, but nevertheless; I'm a big fan of 'seek and ye shall find'. If you look hard enough, you will find some strange thing happen that will confuse you, perhaps even frighten you.

In the end, I'm hoping everyone who reads this book will find it an enjoyable read, a little spooky at times, and a little funny as well. I've tried to provide a little of everything, filling it with scientific theories, true ghost stories, ghost hunts, and historical information. My journey will take place in Southeastern Minnesota, just one tiny location on this planet. Will I find evidence of ghosts? I haven't a clue. But I'm willing to try. In the first few weeks of planning and preparing for this book, I've already become aware of some interesting things happening. Books, cups, and papers flying off shelves and desks, strange footsteps in the night, and faucets turning on by themselves. Odd indeed. Perhaps a poltergeist? A spirit that is trying to communicate with me? I'm not sure. I'm hoping that by the end of this book, I'll have better answers to my questions about life and death.

So join me on this journey of searching for ghosts in Southeastern Minnesota. Come with me while I search for the truth about spirits, ghosts, and ghouls. I've found many interesting stories to work with, locations of historical tragedy and episodes of monumental importance. I promise, the journey will be an adventure, one to curl up with and read each night for fun, helping you on your own real path to believing in ghosts.

A weathered tombstone in one of the many old cemeteries in Southeastern Minnesota.

Contents

Chapter 1
Do You Believe?

"Until you do what you believe in, how do you know whether you believe in it or not?"

—Leo Tolstoy

know I asked in the Foreword, but I'll ask again. Do you believe? It's an important question. I'll give you my answer: I believe in spirit, but I'm not too sure about ghosts. Or perhaps I don't want to know about the ghosts.

I can remember as a young boy how eerie it was making trips into the dark basement for jars of tomatoes. We lived in an old farmhouse that was well over one hundred years old

Ghostly image of phantom person looking out the window of the Anderson House in Wabasha. Other images taken seconds apart did not reveal anyone in the window.

(we knew that because when we remodeled, we found written on the backside of some door trim the words, 'remodeled 1917'). I would tiptoe down the steep limestone steps into the basement, hoping not to disturb any ghosts that lived there. I hoped and prayed the flickering light would stay on (it always did, thankfully). Once finding the tomato jar, I'd race back up the stairs, not wanting to look back and see if any dark shadowy figures were following me. Worse yet, I didn't want any evil demon to grab and pull me down into some secret labyrinth of ghosts and ghouls, never to return to this dimension again.

As you can see, I tend to have a wild imagination. And when it comes to belief, I think we tend to choose our beliefs, based on imagination, along with knowledge and experience. When dealing with the paranormal, our ability to believe is hampered by the lack of concrete evidence—for most of us that is.

There have been millions of people throughout history that believe they have experienced something paranormal. I've had strange things happen to me, but have not spent the time to truly investigate those things—until now that is. I think it's time we dig deeper into the unexplained phenomena happening around us. Perhaps we'll find out that ghosts are everywhere.

But what is this unexplained phenomena? Is it just the wind howling, or a ghost outside our window beckoning to come in? Are the creaking stairs outside the bedroom a ghostly phantom looking for revenge, or just the house settling? It's hard to explain something when you don't know what it is. What is a poltergeist? Or ectoplasm? Or an orb? I hope that we can clear up some of this paranormal jargon in this first chapter.

Paranormal Jargon

First of all, it's important to clarify that the term paranormal encompasses a wide variety of unexplained phenomena. According to the Journal of Parapsychology, paranormal means, "any phenomenon that in one or more respects exceeds the limits of what is deemed physically possible according to current scientific assumptions." In laymen's terms, it means anything unusual that happens but can't be explained by usual science. A few of the paranormal categories are listed below:

Telepathy

Describes the transfer of information on thoughts or feelings between individuals by means other than your five classical senses (sight, hearing, taste, smell, touch).

Extra-Sensory Perception (ESP)

The ability to acquire information by paranormal means, independent of any known physical senses or deduction from previous experience.

Psychokinesis (PK)

Refers to the ability of a person's mind to influence matter, time, space, or energy without the use of any currently known type of physical means.

Reincarnation

Belief that the spirit of a living being survives death to be reborn in a new body.

Ghosts

Apparition or spirit of a deceased person.

Hauntings

Regular occurrence of paranormal phenomena associated with a particular locality, and can include apparitions, poltergeists, cold drafts, footsteps, voices, and odors.

UFOs

Unidentified Flying Objects. Any real or apparent flying object that cannot be identified by the observer.

There are certainly other categories contained in the paranormal catalog, but for this book we want to focus primarily on two categories; Ghosts and Hauntings. More precisely, we want to search for the ghosts and hauntings of Southeastern Minnesota. Through the true ghost stories, and interviewing those who have experienced ghosts firsthand, along with some paranormal investigations of our own, we will hopefully gain a better idea of what ghosts are and how they haunt you. First we should get some basic details on what a ghost is.

What is a Ghost?

It's a simple question, right? A ghost is something that scares the bejeezus out of you. Or, for you adventuresome ghost hunters, it's something that sparks a fire under your passion to explore the unknown. Either way, it would be ideal if we could define what a ghost is more concretely, in terms of its physical (or spiritual) attributes. Of course, that might be difficult since ghosts do not appear to be of this physical world. So what then do we do? All we have is information based on feelings of past experiences by others and ourselves.

Let's analyze a particular paranormal event. If you are one of the lucky ones to have experienced it yourself, great. It will be that much easier. Otherwise, think of a story you've heard. I'll use one of my experiences while growing up, living in the hundred-year-old farmhouse in Farmington, Minnesota. Many strange things happened in and around that house, both good and bad, one event in particular I'll never forget.

I was alone in the house (it always happens like that, doesn't it?). My parents had gone to Wisconsin for the weekend, and my brother was at college, living down in Winona at the time. It was late on a Friday night, around 2 A.M. in the morning. I had just gotten back from a friend's house, and was dead tired (no pun intended). I've never enjoyed being in the house all alone; it always gave me the creeps. At the time, I really wasn't afraid of ghosts and goblins—the thought never entered my mind in fact. I was feeling a little concerned about aliens, having just read Whitley Strieber's *Communion.* I kind of felt like, at some point, the little green men would show up and take me away, but that's another story.

Being the scientific kind of guy that I am (majored in Electronics Engineering and Computer Science), I was aware that there were billions of stars in our galaxy. Furthermore, there are billions of galaxies in our universe. So, odds are that we are not alone. This always sat in the back of my mind (back when I had time to think about such things). I always wondered what it would be like to meet an alien, although I really didn't want to go through the experience.

So there I was, all alone in this drafty old farmhouse at 2 A.M. in the morning. I actually contemplated not staying there, heading all the way back down to Rochester. The rational side of my brain convinced me that sleep was a good thing at the moment, and that there were no such things as aliens, let alone ghosts.

The minute I walked into the house I felt creepy. Everything was dark and very quiet. I quickly flipped on the light switch and sat down in the living room. After a few minutes of channel surfing (on the five network channels back then, pre-satellite/cable days), I decided to get some sleep.

What's interesting is that when I turned off the lights, I immediately sensed something odd was going to happen. Something spooky. All I could think about were the aliens that were probably outside the window, waiting for me to fall asleep and take me away. I was still not worried about the paranormal, just my own silly paranoia. Eventually, I shook my head, rolled over on the couch, and tried to sleep. I could have gone upstairs in my own bed (still there for me even while in college), but I felt safer crashing on the couch.

No sooner had I rolled over when I heard footsteps. Tiny steps, like something small was walking around in the room. Talk about freaky. I tried to ignore them, thinking it was just my mind playing tricks on me. But I kept thinking those aliens were in the house! I turned back to look around the room, with the only light coming from the full moon outside. The footsteps stopped, and of course I saw nothing. I rolled back over to try more sleep, but the footsteps came back, sounding like they were lightly tiptoeing right up to me.

At this point, fear hit hard and I did the only safe thing—pull the blanket up over my head. Yeah, right. That'll stop an alien. Demon trolls, too. Yeah, right.

I continued to hear footsteps walking around the room, and then some really weird sound outside the house. To this day, I have no idea what it was. Sounded like electricity, or a high-pitched motor. We lived out in the country, with our closest neighbor a half a mile away. And just when I shrugged off the outside noise, WHAM! Something moved in the family room.

I bolted for the light switch, not sure what I'd find on my way over to it. Thankfully, I found nothing. With the light switch on, I saw that a picture had fallen over that was leaning against the wall. We had been doing some remodeling in the room and two family pictures were on the floor, leaning up against the wall. One picture had tipped over, the other had not. That was enough for me. I flipped the light switch off and ran for the car. Needless to say, I was quite awake for the hour drive down to Rochester.

So what really happened to me that night? How can I logically and rationally explain the episode? The quickest and easiest way to explain it would be to say I imagined it all. Which is always a possibility when you lack any physical evidence. But assuming I didn't fabricate the whole thing in my mind, just to get a dose of midnight adrenaline, then what did happen?

The first thing that the human mind seems to try to do is explain and categorize things. So, let's look at that. Exhibit A. Old farmhouse with lots of creaks and drafts, not to mention mice. It's easy to say that a mouse was hopping around the room while I tried to sleep, and with it being so quiet I could hear him jumping around on the carpet. The mouse could have also knocked over the picture. And the sound outside the house, it could have been a late night snowmobile (this happened in January), its rider racing home for some sleep.

I've tried to be logical about it, and can assume a mouse was in the room. And a snowmobile outside. But I can't explain how the picture decided to fall at that very moment. Something had to have pushed it over. Why didn't it happen some other time? In order to keep some sanity, my mind tends to just gloss over the event. I really don't dwell on it much. It's as if my mind can't logically categorize the event, so it wants to pretend it didn't happen. But the inquisitive portion of my mind won't let that occur. It knows something strange happened. And it also knows it might happen again.

Let's move forward with the assumption that strange things happen, and that ghosts exist. I'm convinced something moved around in the living room that night, and something moved the picture frame. In some paranormal way, energy may have been used to alter some of the things in the room. If there's one rule to stick with, whether we talk about ghosts or bowling balls, some type of energy must be used in order for us to perceive it. I heard footsteps on the carpet; therefore something actually walked across the carpet (option A), but hid when I peered into the darkness. Or something projected into my mind the awareness that a thing walked across the carpet (option B). Of course, a third option would be that I imagined the entire thing, but we've already decided to ignore that possibility. Otherwise there's no point in reading this book!

Option B is the easiest one to explain, but the hardest to prove. Having a ghost plant the thought of it haunting you leaves no evidence, other than what's in your mind. The only hope of sanity for you is if someone else is there who also got the thought implanted in their mind. To make matters worse, all the instruments and measurements you take will never capture the image broadcasted in your mind, at least not with current instruments. Perhaps there will be some Electrocardiogram (EKG) device or Alpha Beta Theta brainwave device that will capture information as it erupts into the haunted area. Until then, ghosts using option B seem impossible to prove.

Therefore, we are left with option A, where something actually manifested in the room, walked across the floor, and tipped over a picture. With this option, we should be able to capture real, physical evidence that something was there. In this case, we could use cameras, audio recorders, or electromagnetic field (EMF) devices to capture the incident. That is unless the ghost is capable of cloaking its physical manifestation from the recording equipment, which seems highly unlikely to me. Although being that we are dealing with the supernatural, who knows what the ghosts could hide from us. And why are the ghosts revealing anything at all to us?

Now we arrive at an interesting question; why do we have ghosts? What purpose do they have? I'm a big fan of knowing everything has a purpose—everything has a reason to live (and haunt for that matter). To me, ghosts must be attempting to communicate, trying to talk with us about an event that has occurred, is occurring, or will occur in the future. It could be a warning of a future event, or perhaps a tragic happening in the past. Now we're getting somewhere. Ghosts might be thought of as a communication of an extreme event, either catastrophic or perhaps something totally blissful. Perhaps there is a tipping point in our bucket of spiritual awareness, where eventually it becomes too full and spills out into our world in a supernatural way.

The assumption is that ghosts come from spirits or the spirit world (wherever that is!). But then so do we, right? Unless you are an atheist, you believe that this world is only a stepping-stone among others. Everything is spirit to some extent, whether the spirit is a manifestation of a specific entity, or a reflection of our own spirit. Each breath you take and word you read in this book comes ultimately from your spirit. Sure, I wrote the words in this book, but you're reading them now, as an expression of your spirit. Your spirit has decided that reading this book is important, so your mind and body do the diligent task of going to a bookstore (or library), buying the book (or checking it out), curling up on your couch, and reading it. Why would we think that ghosts in the form of spirits are doing anything different? Keep in mind this is only my opinion. If you do not believe in spirit, or some deeper level of energy, then there's no point in thinking about this too much.

Digging deeper into the mystery of ghosts (a.k.a. spirit), we start to recognize that there may be some underlying energy force wanting to experience life, or be experienced. There is some level of intention out there. The power of intention is great, so great that it could be the reason supernatural events happen. Yes, those déjà vu situations that pop into your head once in awhile, or times you and someone else simultaneously say the same thing or think the same thing. It also includes seeing into the future (clairvoyance). I've experienced, to some extent, all three. It's very fascinating when it occurs, yet creepy when you try to figure out how it happens.

It seems to me that ghosts, existing as spirit, have some form of intention. They intend to communicate information about themselves to you. They may provide a continuous replay of a particular event in the past, or even sometimes the future (residual haunting). The key point here is that for unknown reasons, the level of spirit energy is intensified, so much so that it spills over into our world. This is usually caused by some horrific tragedy, or an incredible amount of joy.

But what triggers the ghostly appearance? Are they always floating around, even when we're not there? In my opinion, there has to be a catalyst involved, someone or something that triggers the event. This leads us to another important item involving our own spirit. It seems that our very own spirit can be the catalyst that makes the paranormal event occur. It's also interesting to think that if you're not willing to experience the supernatural, it may not occur at all. It's sort of like having a bad aura, where your negative energy cancels out the energy of the spirit trying to communicate. It seems as though having strong, positive emotions and spiritual energy is critical to experiencing the paranormal. With the supernatural energy in some locations extremely high, all that may be needed is another spirit to add to it and the manifestation may occur.

What may be happening is that ghosts have intentions, and we have intentions, and the combination of the two can bring paranormal manifestations. It's all speculative of course. But it may very well be part of the equation. The events do not happen in the spiritual world, or at least it's beyond our scientific capabilities to record such actions. We occasionally see it in our physical world, or perhaps at least in our mind. In recent history, we have captured volumes of information in the form of pictures and recordings, and on occasion a ghostly figure or voice is found. But are they real? Can we prove once and for all that ghosts exist? Sadly, it seems we cannot. Perhaps with the tremendous amount of video and audio being captured in today's technological world, we will begin to find increasingly strange things recorded. Wouldn't it be nice to start seeing a map of evidence showing the existence of ghosts?

I don't want to burst your bubble, but it seems that no matter how much evidence we find, there's most always a logical explanation. Or at least one cannot verify the evidence has not been tampered with. It seems as though personal experience is still the only true way to convert the nonbelievers. I hope that the stories in this book, and investigations described, may start you down the right path to opening you mind. You may find yourself thinking, well, maybe there's more to life than what I see and understand. Be careful, though. You might not like what you find. Those bumps in the night might be more than just the house settling. And that brush against your shoulder late at night might not be the wind.

If you open your mind, your eyes and ears may start to see and hear things. More importantly, your mind may begin to process things differently, making you think a little harder about what you experience. You may find yourself seeing and hearing the ghosts. As for myself, I've never seen a full apparition, floating down the staircase at midnight while I'm getting a glass of water. Then again, I really don't think I want that kind of experience.

Which leads us back to the power of intention. I intend not to find a creepy ghost floating around my house at midnight. But I do intend to be open to experiencing strange occurrences such as moving objects, mysterious footsteps on the carpet, clairvoyance happenings, and déjà vu. What are your intentions with ghosts? Are you a skeptic or believer? At what point will you look at crossing over to the other side? What's interesting is that in the past few decades, science is catching up with the unexplained paranormal events that occur. Through the understanding of quantum mechanics, we can begin to see that our intention is a key element in the universe we live in.

Quantum mechanics, or quantum physics, has to do with the science of tiny packets of energy called quanta. Essentially, we are talking about quantities of energy and how they act and react in our known universe. Theories and proofs on quantum physics started back in the early twentieth century, when Einstein's Special Theory of Relativity was in full form (once everybody grasped its concept). Major breakthroughs in science were occurring because of his bridging the gap between the old Newtonian physics (that explain much of the normal world we live in), and the unexplainable measurements of the atomic world.

The scientific community was quite happy with the theories, but there were still some mysterious measurements when looking deep into the mechanism of an atom. The particles within the atom behave very strangely indeed, popping in and out of existence. In fact, with the Heisenberg Uncertainty Principle, it was explained that you could never know exactly where a particle was located (position), and where it was going (momentum). With this in mind, probability was used to calculate the action of the particles, and thus entered the world of quantum physics.

Another interesting part of quantum mechanics deals with how the observer alters the outcome of a scientific measurement.

For instance, if I want to measure a photon with an electron microscope, the electrons hitting the photon will change their location and momentum. Similarly, there's a famous thought experiment (hopefully in thought only) called Schrödinger's Cat, where a feline is placed in a box with a device that would randomly emit an amount of poison to kill the cat. Since the device emitting the poison was random, the cat may or may not be alive when you open the box. Quantum physics indicates the cat in the box is both alive and dead; the actual result will be determined when you open the box. With the cat's life hanging by a poisoned thread, you wonder if perhaps the observer opening the box influences the fate of the feline inside. Could the intention of the observer change the results of what's inside the box when you open it? Some physicists believe so.

And one final thought on quantum physics; scientists have actually been able to show that time travel is possible. Okay, not like in *Star Trek*, or *Quantum Leap*, but at least in the particle realm. Scientists setup an experiment to send a photon from a laser through a series of mirrors, splitting the photon into two paths. The experiment gets quite technical, but it has to do with the Heisenberg Uncertainty Principle, in that the split photon particles influence each other, regardless of their distance (also known as entanglement). It's like the split photon particles can communicate instantaneously with each other. This would infer that there is some external dimension, outside of our time and space, in which the particles are communicating. This 'spooky action at a distance' as Einstein called it, proves there is some mysterious level of existence beyond our dimension. Could that level include ghosts?

If you're interested in finding out more about quantum physics, Heisenberg's Uncertainty Principle, and Schrödinger's Cat, go nuts. There are tons of books on the subjects, but I'm not going to bore you anymore on the details. It's enough to say right now that with quantum physics, you have packets of energy popping in and out of our time-space continuum. That intrigues me, because it sounds very similar to what ghosts do.

The energy of a ghost pops into our dimension from the spirit world dimension, and then pops back out. What's interesting too is that there may be a probability of 'ghost energy', popping in at a particular location. Perhaps there's a way to predict when a ghost will appear.

So could ghostly activity be the by-product of some quantum fluctuation in our space-time continuum? Possibly. Which could also explain why our equipment to measure the activity does not capture anything. Typical ghost hunting devices are not capable of measuring events at the quantum level; they cannot record the location and momentum of quantum energy. Our minds, however, might be capable of 'seeing' the events, even when our physical video and audio recording equipment cannot.

I hope this chapter has opened your mind a little. Perhaps now you see that there might be more to this world then you originally thought. From now on maybe you'll keep a closer eye on the things that go bump in the night, and the footsteps in the hallway. Who knows, you might actually see something you can't explain. Then what will you do? Will you believe? Only time will tell—and more paranormal experiences.

Chapter 2
Journey into Spirit

"Great spirits have always encountered violent opposition from mediocre minds."

—Albert Einstein

Clouds rolling in on the suburbs of Rochester, perhaps bringing ghostly spirits with them.

art of the process in having ghost stories is not only to read them, but to also try to understand them. At least the real ghost stories, which is what's gathered in this book. After reading other books, interviewing witnesses or those that have been told the ghostly tale, I decided to take things one step further. Kick it up a notch as it were. I decided to do a little investigating myself. Sure, I'm no expert in the field, but I do enjoy the topic of ghosts, and have read many books over the years on the subject. And I believe I've been haunted once or twice in the past, or at least seen things I can't explain. Experience + knowledge = professional, right? Qualified or not, ghost hunting sounds like fun. I'm just not sure what to do if I bump into one. Screaming will most likely be an option. Running away is probably even better.

Historically speaking, most ghost stories are handed down verbally from generation to generation. They were the spooky tales told and acted out around a campfire, or in the house right before bedtime. What a fantastic way to fall asleep—scared out of your wits. Go figure. Still, that's what was done. In time, we grew up and cast the tall tales aside, thinking of them as that, fictitious articles of imagination. But were they? Was there any truth to them?

The ghost stories wouldn't fade away. We grew up, but the stories still stayed. And there seems to always be new stories to tell—ones that are supposedly real. As an adult, it can become hard to believe in the magic and supernatural. In fact, most of us shrug off the unexplained events we hear about, assuming they're from some lunatic involved with hallucinogenic drugs or bad apple pie late at night. But every once in a while, one of the nonbelievers gets converted into a believer—not because they want to, but because of their being confronted with firsthand experience of the paranormal. They walk away from the ordeal knowing that ghosts exist.

Wouldn't it be nice to wake up one day and read the headlines in a newspaper stating, "Proof that ghosts exist!" That would grab your attention. But how do we prove that they exist? Well, at a basic level, we have to find a way to measure them. Once that is done, we can capture the measurements and show them to the rest of the world. The problem is that ghosts seem to be very good at hiding themselves and any evidence that they have haunted you. More precisely, they make it impossible for the evidence to be captured in a way that provides absolute proof. It's like the ghosts 'sort of' want us to recognize them, but not enough to make it obvious. Perhaps it's all a game to them, to see which ghost can 'almost' convince you that they exist.

As I indicated, the key to being able to having a newspaper claiming that ghosts exist has to do with capturing absolute proof. The only way that will happen is if we take measurements of haunted places. And the more spooky places we monitor, the more evidence should show up. The more the merrier. Just imagine if we had millions of people routinely inspecting haunted buildings. A web site could be created for us to download the evidence for all to see. Eventually, we would discover a pattern, and the newspaper article claiming that ghosts exist would soon follow. That is of course if the ghosts don't hack the web site.

The proof will be in the ectoplasm pudding. If we get enough investigators, we should begin to see the pattern. But what techniques do we use to capture evidence of ghosts? I've listed below some of the equipment you can use. Depending on your level of ghost hunting, some of the equipment may or may not be necessary. In the end, having an audio recorder and camera is about all you need. Obviously, the more equipment you have, measuring a wider range of the environment, the better your chances are of capturing proof of the supernatural activity. Perhaps bombarding the ghost with a plethora of recording devices will make it slip up and not alter or hide the evidence, right? I can just see a ghost frantically running around to a hundred audio recorders in a room after scaring the pants off a group of investigators.

Air Ion Counter

Used to detect natural and artificial ions. Natural ions come from the decay of radioactive minerals and radon gas, ions generated by fire, lightning, and storm activity. The theory is that paranormal events will generate electrical activity, or radiation, thereby creating an ionic discharge into the room you are investigating. It can also be associated with why your hair stands up when a ghostly apparition enters the room.

Bags

Seems silly to mention, but you should have some gallon-sized airtight freezer bags, to bring specimens (coin or book that moved, ectoplasm, etc.) back to your lab (a.k.a garage) to analyze it.

Barometer

Used to measure atmospheric pressure. A sudden drop (or rise) in barometric pressure could be a sign of some localized anomaly (such as a ghost), or more commonly that the weather's changing.

Camera

The quintessential device used to capture the ghost in action. More recently, digital cameras are being used and allow you to take hundreds of shots. Digital video cameras are great too—not only for the pictures (especially if you have night vision capabilities), but also for the audio.

Candles and Matches

Obviously used for light—especially when your flashlight batteries go dead due to paranormal activity, or just plain forgetting to replace them. Of course, who says the ghost wouldn't blow out your candle?

Compass

A dual-purpose device. One is for monitoring magnetic fluctuations that paranormal activity may induce. The other (more important in my opinion) is to help you navigate your way back to your car if lost out in a large cemetery.

Digital Audio Recorder

My personal favorite. A simple device used to capture anomalies in the audio frequency range. Great to have several of these running to be used as secondary measurements. I've named mine. It's called D.A.R.R.E.N. which stands for Digital Audio Recorder of Really Eerie Noises.

Dowsing Rods

One or two rods bent in an 'L' or 'Y' shape that you hold in your hands that supposedly help you find things. I keep a miniature dowsing rod in my back pocket for when I loose my car keys.

EMF Detector

An ElectroMagnetic Field Detector measures electromagnetic radiation. This device is a standard for most ghost hunting teams, under the assumption that apparitions give off electromagnetic radiation.

Extra Batteries

A no brainer. Especially needed for the poltergeist that loves to drain the batteries in your flashlight. Although I'm not sure why the poltergeist wouldn't drain the power in the extra batteries.

Flash Lights

Yep. Always needed while hunting ghosts. I'd bring several of them if I were you. Ones that clip to your hat work great.

First Aid Kit

This is a must. Not so much for aiding you after a poltergeist attack, but for patching you up after running around in the dark, bumping into tables, or walking into a tree while your night-vision goggles go on the blink.

Geiger Counters

Used to detect gas-ionization fluctuations in Alpha, Beta, Gamma, and X-ray radiation levels, which can be present during ghostly encounters. But it can also mean you're standing in a location full of dangerous radiation, which is not a good thing.

Ghost Catcher (a.k.a. Spirit Wind Chime)

This helps you catch wind movement, hopefully generated by paranormal activity. Basically any wind chime will do, or any thing that can easily be moved. No sense in making the ghost work too hard.

Headset Communications

Great to have for communicating between team members. They free up your hands for the recording equipment, and for dodging the occasional flying object from a poltergeist.

Infrared Thermal Scanner

This device allows you to measure 'cold spots', where an object or location in a room is much colder than the rest. But the chilling spot may just be from an open window or cold air return instead of the supernatural.

Mobile phone

More for an emergency, rather than communicating with ghosts. Although there are cases in which spooky voices have been heard on cell phones. Yes, a haunting, "Can you hear me now?" would be creepy indeed.

Motion Detectors

These devices detect motion, and are great for monitoring if people walk into a location, or to wake you up if a ghost has snuck in.

Night Vision Equipment

This equipment is great for seeing things that go bump in the night. But it can be a bit expensive.

Notebook

A small pad of paper and a pen is instrumental during the initial investigation. But a digital recorder in my opinion works just as good. As long as you have something to jot down notes as well, mainly the time at which events occur.

Thermometer

Not the kind you stick in your mouth. It's a basic room thermometer to check on drastic temperature changes. Paranormal activity can sometimes send chills not only through your spine, but also through the room. See infrared thermal scanner.

Wristwatch

Critical piece of equipment to make sure you keep on track during your investigation and to record when you stumble on the unusual events. It's also good to have a watch with an alarm, in case you end up dozing while waiting for the ghosts to appear.

As you can see, there are tons of equipment options for you while searching for ghosts. It just depends to what degree you want proof. Bombarding the specter with dozens of recording devices should give you a better chance at catching the event, right? Possibly. In my opinion, it depends on two things: how smart the ghost is, and how much control it has in leaving traces.

In terms of figuring out how smart a ghost is, that's up for grabs. I would think that being clever has less to do with it. Just because you're smart doesn't always give you the go ahead to do what ever you want. There should still be some basic boundaries in which that ghost must operate in. There must be reasons why the ghost shows up. With that in mind, we can then formulate why the ghost appears, and then possibly discover ways to record its activity.

To me, the most logical (if there's logic involved at all with ghosts) idea is that the ghost must follow certain rules for haunting. In particular, I believe that it cannot easily manifest itself physically into our dimension—not at least without an immense amount of power. And if it does not easily show up physically in our dimension, it would not be too easy to record its activity. It's as if the ghost 'wants' to be recorded, not that it was dumb enough or foolish enough to leave behind a trace.

Let's face it; it seems like we only become aware of the ghosts when they want us to be aware. Countless hours of investigation by ghost hunters have turned up little to no concrete evidence. Once in a while we'll get an orb (ball of energy), or a sudden change in temperature or EMF. But getting a full-fledged apparition to dance an Irish jig in front of you? Hasn't happened that I'm aware of—not recorded on video that is. Still, occasionally there are brief glimpses of shadowy figures and unknown voices. And objects moving by themselves. Even with this, the skeptic will claim someone has tampered with the video. Even if nobody tampered with the tape, you never find a clear picture of some ghostly apparition. Whatever energy is being produced, its source is never clearly known.

I'm not doubting the existence of ghosts, just the ability to capture it on tape. Like I said before, it's almost as if the ghost decides when and where it will be noticed. We have no control over it (except if you believe you are a catalyst, making the ghost appear). So setting up a ton of ghost hunting equipment may or may not help. Better yet, having all that recording going on may inhibit the ability for the ghost to show up. There may be some ghost rules that say, "Thou shall not manifest if thy human has more than three measuring devices." It makes you wonder what sort of intelligence we are dealing with. Sure seems like a lot of intelligence, to be able to exist and not be caught on tape, especially with all the video and audio being taken in the world today.

Perhaps it is too difficult for the ghost to alter the recording equipment if there are too many of them. My thought is that one device is all you need. It might make the ghost bolder in its debut with you. In the amateurish paranormal investigations I have done for this book, I used my digital camera and my ICD-P520 digital audio recorder (as I mentioned, I call my digital recorder D.A.R.R.E.N.—Digital Audio Recorder of Really Eerie Noises). That's all I need in my opinion. Everything else (besides flashlight and first aid) is just extra gravy. Sure, I'm not going to catch temperature fluctuations and ionic discharges as the ghost appears, or notice high levels of EMF as it enters our dimension. But if the ghost shows up, I will hopefully get a few pictures and some mysterious voices recorded.

I'm really not asking for the ghost world to ring a thousand bells and sing the Alleluia chorus. Just a little audio proof is good enough for me. If I can get a blurry shadow, a buzzing sound where it shouldn't be, or a phantom voice mumbling something when I know the room is quiet, I'm good to go.

That's enough proof for me. It's not as if I'm trying to find irrefutable proof; I don't expect to capture the evidence that will change the world. I just want to change *my* world, to find out once and for all if there truly are ghosts.

The other thing I like about this minimalistic approach to ghost hunting, is that anyone can do it. And at any time. That's the key in my opinion. I think if we can get thousands of people recording audio sounds (and pictures) in spooky places, we should have lots of proof to convert a few more nonbelievers. And it doesn't have to be specifically for finding ghosts. You may have recorded some audio at a recent business meeting seminar. Why not listen to the recording for any strange sounds? Just don't take pictures while you're at it. It will probably get you kicked out.

The other key factor is to make sure you have an open mind. Like I've said, I'm a big fan of 'ask and ye shall receive'. Basically, if you don't want to believe, than in most cases you won't. The opposite is true as well, where wanting to believe should eventually produce some results. And for the group on the fence, between believing and non-believing, just open your mind and listen. I think you might be surprised at what you see and hear.

An important note on ghost hunting—make sure you are always respectful of privacy. Never be on private property without permission. And always ask about taking pictures, video, or audio. Most people are fine with audio, and it works well for keeping notes too. After getting proper approval, you can wander through a building with your audio recording, talking to it and asking questions (to the spirit world of course), and taking notes in it. And to prevent being annoying, sometimes you may want to keep the recorder in your shirt pocket as you walk around. Sort of trying to sneak up on the ghost, like you're in stealth mode. You'll get a lot of interference from the rustling in your shirt pocket, but I figure if the ghost wants to talk, he'll let you know. If the hair on the back of your neck starts standing up, that's a good time to pull out your recorder.

I hardly call my version of investigation true ghost hunting. There are many organizations that take it very seriously, using loads of equipment, and have been doing it for years. Still, I'm looking for basic paranormal activity, and even if it's just my own little head that's recording the event, it's still good for me. In the end, your own mind and sensations can be the best way to measure paranormal activity. Yes, I know it makes it hard to take the measurement and give it to somebody else to analyze. But at least you won't be a skeptic anymore. You'll have firsthand experience, even if you can't prove it.

The other thing to remember is to never go out investigating by yourself. And it's not so much that you can be hurt by the ghosts (although that can happen), but that a real person or persons might harm you, mugging you or doing worse things. The last thing you want is to become the ghost by being in the wrong place at the wrong time!

Whatever way you take on your journey into the spirit world, try to do it with an open mind. Look at the world around you in a different way—see that it is a world filled with spirit. Everything that exists, stems from spirit, whether it is a paranormal event from the extra-dimension, or an everyday occurrence such as walking the dog, it's still all spirit. Take a few minutes out of each day and look around you—see the spirit floating from one point to the next. Understand that life is just one neverending journey into spirit.

Most of the remainder of the book delves into the true ghost stories that I've found by interviewing others or capturing information via email and Internet. All of the stories are real, or at least the paranormal activity is. In some cases, I've condensed the activity into one night, or modified the person experiencing the events to protect their identity. After each true ghost story I have a historical section that describes exactly what events had occurred, based on the information I received. Lastly, I've done some investigating myself, and have included that after the historical section. I hope that you will enjoy the stories, be captured by the actual history, and anxious with the investigations. I know I was!

Chapter 3
Interview with A Ghost

"She scares me. I know that sounds odd, but even a ghost can get scared of another ghost."

Old farmhouse similar to the one the Jensens built back in the mid 1800s.

Location: Albert Lea

I t's not an easy thing being a ghost. Sure, it has its benefits. You never get hungry, and you never get hurt. But I'd rather be real. Oh, to make bread one more time, rolling the flour out, baking it in the oven. Or to smell the white daffodils out front in the planters hanging on the porch. I'd even enjoy sweeping and cleaning the house—anything to have a taste of being real once again.

I try to be quiet, silently floating from room to room in the Borland House. But every now and then one of the Borland children get out of hand. It spooks me, making me become visible for a moment. The next thing I know they're staring at me, whiter than a ghost like me.

The rambling farmhouse I haunt used to be mine, way back in the early 1900s. My husband, James, built it with his own hands. A lot of love poured into this house. And now it's owned by the Borlands. Good for them. They're a nice family. I don't mind sharing it with them. It's better than having the house stand empty. Or having all those other families here. I didn't like them here. The lady upstairs hated them too. She's the one that drove them out.

James and I loved this house. I especially did. Perhaps that's why I can't leave. I have so many pleasant memories wrapped up within these walls. The parties, the friends, the families. They're all still here. I couldn't possibly leave. All of the recollections are so wonderful. All except the ones with that ghostly lady upstairs.

James noticed her right away. He'd barely been done building the house when her apparition showed up. I eventually saw her too and was not at all pleased. The lady seemed evil; you felt all dark and gloomy when she appeared. Thankfully, she spent all of her time upstairs, most of it in the back southwest bedroom. We ended up not using that room. I suppose she claimed it for herself. James thought she was the wife from the farmer in the log cabin that lived on this land before he built the house. But we never figured out for sure why she haunted the place.

You would think now that I'm a ghost too, I could find out more about the lady upstairs. I can't, or at least I won't. I still stay away from her. She scares me. I know that sounds odd, but even a ghost can get scared of another ghost.

Most of my time is spent watching and wishing. I watch the Borland kids, making sure they're safe. There were countless times I had to step in and save them from things like a broken arm, influenza, and even a burglar. I felt it to be my job, taking care of them, and making sure the lady upstairs doesn't frighten them too much.

I keep wishing to move on, but it doesn't seem to happen. I'm torn between a new life in heaven, and my old life in this home. I just can't leave it. The house is who I am. Perhaps someday I'll see the sun rise and decide it's time. Until then, I've got a job to do, protecting the people who live in the house from harm, and protecting the house itself. And maybe someday the spooky lady upstairs will go away. Then I can enjoy my house from top to bottom. And perhaps then I can leave, moving on to be with my husband, James.

History:

The ghost depicted in the story above is Grandma Jensen, which was discussed in the *Haunted Heartland* book by Beth Scott and Michael Norman. Most people know the house as the Borland House in Albert Lea. I thought it might be fun to tell the story from the ghost's point of view.

The two-story farmhouse was built back in 1893 by James Jensen on the south side of Albert Lea. Right away Mr. Jensen knew something was wrong. He noticed the presence of a ghost upstairs in the south bedroom. It was definitely a restless soul wandering around in the room, and making him feel like someone was always looking over his shoulder.

The Jensen family lived in the house for fifty-three years, moving out in 1946. In all the years they lived there, they stayed away from the south bedroom, never wanting to spend much time in it. And over the years since the Jensen family lived there, fourteen other families have moved in, but quickly moved out. They felt like they were being driven from the house by some unknown presence.

The house stood vacant for a few years, until in 1964, the Borland family moved in. With nine children in the family, there was much excitement. Too much excitement apparently, especially when within a couple weeks the children noticed the figure of a tall, thin woman in a flowered dress appear upstairs near the south bedroom. The children ran to tell their mother, who did not believe them at first. Not until she saw the woman a few weeks later.

Sometimes the ghost could also be seen on a balcony outside the room, or in the second floor hallway. Occasionally, she would even be seen walking into the south bedroom closet, only to vanish into the darkness.

Eventually, the Borland family realized that south bedroom was haunted. They decided to stay away from the room, not wanting to sleep or do anything in the room. They left the room to the phantom lady, and she rarely bothered them from then on.

Some research has been done on the location of the house, and it was determined that the property was homesteaded with a log cabin built back in the early to mid 1850s. Perhaps the upstairs ghost is that of the lady who lived there. What's interesting is that the lady never goes downstairs. But there is a ghost on the main floor of the house.

The ghostly apparition on the main floor is that of an elderly lady. She is pleasant, always running around as if too many things were needing to be done. She spent a great deal of time in the kitchen area where a pantry used to be located, busy shuffling along as if making dinner or baking bread.

One other interesting fact about the house is that it apparently was used as the basis for a *Happy Days* TV episode (from 1970s) about a haunted house. It was also used in an episode of *Little House on the Prairie*.

Chapter 4
Chimney Portal

"You never get used to waking up at night and finding a troll coming out of your closet…"

House in Cannon Falls, possibly containing a portal into other worlds.

Location: Cannon Falls

t first started when I was nine months old. I could see the thing through a mirror in my room as I stood at the end of the crib. I'll never forget how terrified I was, seeing the short little troll-like creature running around my room, with gnarled face, beady red eyes, and razor-sharp finger nails. I screamed. My mother came in, but she could not see it. Still, the scream helped as the troll left the room. But not for long.

A few years had passed but my memory of the troll was as sharp as ever. I had just turned five years old, and could tell there was something strange going on in the house. I was sure the troll was back again. Footsteps in the middle of the night became a common occurrence. I could handle the footsteps; that didn't bother me. It was the beady red eyes staring at me through the slats in my closet door.

The door to my closet had slats across it. I was told that lets the clothes in the closet breathe and stay fresh. What they didn't realize was that it let the trolls breathe too. And stare at me through the slats. I'll tell you right now, there's nothing more scary than waking up at night, having the feeling someone's watching you, only to roll over and see two beady red eyes looking at you down low through your closet door. Well, there is one thing even scarier than that. Having those two beady red eyes staring at you from along side your bed is worse.

I would have been quite happy with the troll staying in the closet. Beady red eyes and all. But they didn't stay there. One night I could hear something prancing around in the room, most likely walking from the closet to my bed, or over to the door to the hallway. The next night I could tell, something was pacing back and forth around my bed from one side to the other. I eventually got up enough nerve to open my eyes. I really don't recommend doing that. It's only going to terrify you.

Slowly opening my eyes, I peered across my bed toward the closet door. No beady red eyes. Good. But I still had that feeling something was watching me. I looked down at the foot of my bed, not wanting to find anything. Thankfully, I didn't. Feeling a bit better, I rolled over opposite the closet door. Bad idea. That's when I saw it.

There's nothing like staring down a troll, point blank. It was inches from my face. I could feel its stinky breath on me. Its beady red eyes, framed around a gnarling leather-skinned face and wide grin, stared at me, as if waiting for me to scream. I didn't disappoint it.

There are light, dainty screams, the kind you make when you're really not that scared, more just alarmed than anything. Then there's the heavy blood-curdling screams. That's what I yelled. It did the trick. In an instant, the troll was gone. My mom came rushing into the room, expecting to find me dead by the way I screamed. I told her about the troll. What surprised me even more was that she understood.

What I didn't realize was that my mom had her own incidents in the house. Big, tall, shadowy figures roaming from room to room. She could sense they were men, or at least were at one time. She had been visited many times by them, always terrified and never the same afterward. I never saw the tall shadow men; the trolls were enough for me.

I began to wonder if there was something about the house, or perhaps the location of it. The house had been around for over one hundred years. Its located just off East Park in Cannon Falls. It doesn't seem like a house that would have a connection to other worlds. But it does. We had a psychic stop by and check things out at one point. She immediately knew there was a presence here. Lots of them as a matter of fact. Eventually she concluded that the house has a portal in it, a doorway to worlds from other dimensions. That would explain the ugly troll problem and tall shadow men.

As it turns out, there's this old chimney that runs up and down through the house. The rooms that have the most activity have the chimney running through it. We figured that's where the trolls are coming from. That's when I made it a point to have my dad crank the heat up at night. Not just to stay warmer in the chilly Minnesota winters, more importantly to try to burn the trolls, or at least smoke them out. Unfortunately, it didn't help. If anything, it only made them angrier.

We had the other usual annoyances in the haunted house: moving tables, moving chairs, clocks taken off the wall. The funniest incident was when my mother put a mousetrap behind the oven. Later that night she heard a commotion in the kitchen. She went in to see what was making all the noise, but found nothing. The next day she reached into one of the kitchen drawers and found the mousetrap in it, sprung. I chuckled to think about some poor troll sneaking behind the oven, only to be caught in the mousetrap!

It seems like this paranormal stuff follows me around. I moved out of my parent's house a few years back, moving to a house in Hastings. Within a few weeks, strange things began to happen there too. Cupboard doors opening and closing on their own, and furniture moving around. As it turns out, the house was built where an old house was torn down—one that had a family murdered in it. That could explain the weird things happening.

Wherever I go, I sometimes can feel strange things. Nothing like the trolls in my bedroom closet. But I still feel some strange presence. I don't like to think about the beady red eyes, but sometimes I wake up at night, wondering if the eyes will be there, staring at me and waiting for me to scream.

History:

I pulled into the McDonalds in Cannon Falls and waited to interview a mother and daughter who had experienced some strange things in a house they lived in near Eastside Park. I was expecting a few annoying ghosts turning lights on and off. Perhaps even the occasional car keys or book being mysteriously misplaced. I wasn't prepared for trolls.

The key element in the one-hundred-plus-year-old house was this chimney running through it. They repeatedly made a comment about it, as if perhaps it was a portal into other worlds. Yes, portal, and other worlds. That's apparently where the trolls were coming from. Short little guys, staring at you from the slats in the door of your closet. Can't get much creepier than that. Unless they came out once and awhile and hung out at the foot of your bed. Which is what they liked to do to the daughter.

Not just the end of your bed, but they also liked to stand on the side of the bed, staring at you inches from your face while you slept, or tried to sleep. I'm thinking I'd be changing the sheets on my bed quite often in that house. Not to mention my pajamas. There's two things that really creep me out: dolls and trolls. I can handle the poltergeist activity (for the most part), and the occasional shadowy thing out of the corner of my eye. But staring point plank at a troll with beady red eyes, or a doll grinning at me, would be just too much.

As I said, the rooms that were connected to a chimney going through the house seemed to have the most activity. That was where the daughter and her sister stayed. Both of them have experienced the trolls. They would hear them walking around at night from one side of the bed to the other. It started at a young age; the daughter remembers seeing the troll at nine months old. Later, at five years of age, she started seeing it more frequently, and closer to her. Screaming was her best defense, for every time she screamed when she saw one, it would disappear.

The mother was not left out of the excitement. She never saw trolls, but instead saw very tall shadowy figures. She felt they were men, and were not at all too friendly. Several times she would find herself confronted with one of them, each time terrified even more than the other times. Eventually, the tall shadow figures would leave, but her memory of them never would. Even though she no longer lives in the house, she worries they will return. She even claims to have taken a picture of a shadow figure. Unfortunately, I did not have the opportunity to see it.

The house itself has had lots of other paranormal activity. Furniture at any given time can be found moved from one location in the house to another. TVs will go on and off without anyone handling the remote. Light switches do the same. And it was a common occurrence to hear footsteps running up and down the hallway late at night. Friends of the daughter during sleepovers have heard the mysterious footsteps as well.

Years ago, a psychic had visited the house. She immediately knew something was wrong. After a few minutes of checking out the place, she concluded that there was a portal in it. Hence the trolls and shadow men. I'm not a big fan of portals, but I suppose they could be like worm holes, allowing you to travel from one location in the universe to another. Perhaps that's just it, these trolls aren't from another dimension, just another part of the universe.

The father has had some interesting things happen as well, including numerous scratches on his body. He would wake up to find himself scratched in various places, perplexed as to how the marks got there.

Overall, the place sounds like there are a lot of things going bump in the night. Gnarly little troll things and tall shadowy things to be exact. It definitely sounds like a place to do an investigation. Just not sure if I'd want to sleep there. Waking up to see beady red eyes staring at me is not something I would look forward to.

Chapter 5
Crack Squad Mischief

*"I don't recommend playing ghostly pranks on your fellow students.
Sometimes they turn out to be real."*

Sketch of the main campus at Shattucks St. Mary's School.

Location: Faribault

I've been going to Shattuck-St. Mary's School in Faribault
for seven years. With several weeks of being in twelfth
grade under my belt, I felt it was time to have some fun
with the ninth graders in middle school. Since it was going to
be Halloween next week, a spooky prank was in order. One that
would send the ninth graders running. What I didn't expect
was that it sent me running too.

"Hey, Patrick," called my friend, Thomas, from down the
hallway of Whipple dorm where we lived on the third floor. "Do
you have everything ready for the big scare Friday night?"

"Keep it down," I replied. "We need to keep it a secret from faculty."

"Good point." He slapped my back and added, "Can't wait to see the looks on their faces when the ghost jumps out at them!"

Thomas was right. It would be fun. I couldn't resist the perfect ghostly prank, especially when it involved the Crack Squad Ghost story. Everyone knew about the story where men in old military uniform would show up at night in your dorm room, quietly standing in the corner watching you.

The tale was a big hit with the students in middle school, and the ninth graders were no exception. They would soon be graduating to the upper campus, excited for the change. Us boys in twelfth grade enjoyed spooking the younger boys; it had become a school tradition. This year would be no different. The basic plan had several crack squad ghosts appearing in my dorm room, while the invited ninth grade boys from St. Mary's Hall south would freak out. Probably wet their pants. That's when the fun would begin. At least that's what the plan was. Apparently nobody told the real ghosts what was supposed to happen.

Carter and his roommate, Charles, were our designated boys; they happen to be two of the most obnoxious individuals in middle school and nearly all of campus. I figured giving them a good fright would knock them down a notch or two. What I didn't plan on was how the whole ordeal ended up knocking me down too. Literally.

With everyone attending an orchestra event Friday night in Newhall Auditorium, Patrick and I had plenty of time to setup our room. There wasn't much to do initially. The main task was hiding the speaker system and fishing line that would help make our ghosts rise up spontaneously during our 'calling of the ghostly Crack Squad'.

Our ghost was made of a navy-blue bed sheet (which we 'found' in Breck Hall where the girls' dorm was) powdered with flour, a coat hanger (from a closet near the dining room in Morgan Hall), and fishing line. It would be wired up so we could pull the line from the opposite side of the room. To the boys it would look like a dark figure had come to life from out of the closet. We tested it out several times. It was guaranteed to send chills through the two boys and have them screaming away.

It wasn't difficult getting Carter and Charles to our third floor dorm room in Whipple. Anytime a student from the middle school got an invitation to visit the upper campus, they jumped at it. Then they could go back to the middle school students and brag about it. But this invitation wasn't something they'd be bragging about, especially if they ended up screaming like little girls.

At 9:30 P.M., there was a knock at our door. I surveyed the room, making sure everything was in its place. With the lights down low, you couldn't see the fishing line high above, or the wires for the speakers by the closet. I smirked at Patrick and opened the door. But there was nobody there. I walked out into the hallway but still could find no one. Then the door to our room slammed shut.

By the time I got back in, Patrick looked spooked, with his face completely white.

"What's up?" I asked. "You don't look so good."

Patrick said, "Yeah, I, ah, don't know. I was sitting here watching you walk out into the hallway, then it seemed like something blew past me. Made me feel very cold, down to the bone. Then the door slammed shut."

"I'm sure it was the wind," I said, although I wasn't entirely sure. Just before the door closed, I felt the same chilling air blow by me. It was too cold, even for October in Minnesota.

No sooner had I closed the door to our room, when there was another knock. This time I slowly opened the door and peeked around the side. It was Carter and Charles. "Hey," I said. "Come on inside." I'm guessing my spooky look around the door at them helped set the mood.

St. Mary's building for the younger grades
at Shattucks St. Mary's School.

We had a table setup, with a makeshift Ouija board sitting on top that Patrick made. Carter and Charles had no idea what they were getting involved with, other than we told them it was sort of initiation for upper campus. They were the lucky ones to be picked.

Carter and Charles looked at each other, not sure if they should be honored or worried. Either way, they were there and ready to go through with it.

"Ever played with a Ouija board?" asked Patrick with a devilish smile.

Both boys shook their heads.

Patrick held the board, shifting it back and forth. "Well, we have. It's lots of fun."

I motioned the two boys to sit down, facing the closet area. Patrick sat on one side and I sat on the other. If everything went right, we'd have a navy-blue bed sheet ghost flying at them in a few minutes. But of course, not everything went right.

Patrick lit a candle on the table, turned off all the other lights, and then explained how to use the board. "All we have to do is put our hands on this plastic thing, ask a question, and it will mysteriously point to the answer. Let's try a practice one. We'll ask a question that we don't know. Like, what is the name of Carter's Mom?"

With everyone's hands on the plastic triangle, it hovered over the letters, S… H… E… L… L… Y.

Carter turned white and said, "That's right. Wow. It really does work."

What we neglected to tell Carter was that we hacked into the school database from Hirst Library and found out his mother's name, along with a bunch of other tidbits of information. We did the same thing for Charles. After several questions, the boys were convinced.

"Now comes the fun part," I said, leaning forward. The candlelight flickering from below my face made it light up with dancing shadows, adding to the eerie ambience. "Let's check on the Crack Squad Ghosts." I cleared my throat and asked,

"Are there any ghosts in the room?" Without even touching the plastic triangle piece, it moved to Y... E... S.

Patrick and I looked at each other. That was not part of the plan. At first I thought maybe Patrick had some extra tricks up his sleeve, somehow making the thing move. But the expression on his face indicated otherwise.

I was a bit spooked out by what had just happened, and wasn't sure if I wanted to continue. Thankfully, Patrick took over. "Oh, great spirits of Shattuck-St. Mary's School. Do we have the Crack Squad Ghosts with us tonight?" The triangle piece instantly moved to Y... E... S, then flew off the table over to the closet. That's when we started hearing the whispering, like a thousand voices were quietly talking among themselves.

The voices would have been a great affect, if we were the ones doing it. But we were not. Patrick thought that maybe I had added a new recording, instead of our scary moaning sounds. But when he checked the switch for the recorder and speakers, and noticed it wasn't on, he got scared too. That's when the dark, shadowy figures appeared by the closet.

I would have much rather preferred navy-blue shadowy figures, but obviously it wasn't an option. This was the real deal. All four of us were freaked out.

The shadows continued to grow. You could see them hovering in place, dancing back and forth, as if ready to pounce any second. That's exactly what they did.

Of course, we couldn't tell that, because the candle blew out. But we could feel them dart at us and circle around right above our heads. All four of us pushed away from the table, sending us backward to the floor. We were screaming too. Big girly screams. I'll admit it. I was frightened and thought I'd have to change my shorts later.

But the incident only lasted maybe fifteen seconds. It felt like eternity. We crawled to the door, opened it, and ran out. It took awhile for Patrick and I to go back in our room. Nothing else strange happened after that. But we learned our lesson. Don't mess with Crack Squad Ghosts. They're real.

The ninth graders had quite the story to take back to the middle school. One of Ouija boards, spooky shadows, and twelfth grade boys screaming like girls. I think this year the joke was on us. That's okay. I'd rather have a joke on me than another one of those ghostly shadows.

History:

Shattuck-St. Mary's School in Faribault is a fantastic school for boys and girls grades six through twelve. They even have a grade thirteen of post-secondary classes for those wishing to include an additional year before heading off to a top-ten college. Shattuck-St. Mary's was originally two schools (hence the name), Shattuck was a boys' school that opened in 1858, and St. Mary's was a school for girls that opened in 1866. In 1972, the schools merged (along with another school, St. James).

Throughout the years, many prestigious families have sent their children to the school. Some students have gone on to become famous individuals, such as actor Marlon Brando. His signature can still be seen written on the green room wall of the theater.

With such a rich history of the schools, going back over 150 years, there is no doubt that there are many possibilities for strange things to occur. Some of the more interesting stories focus on events in buildings such as the Whipple Dormitory, Breck Hall, and St. Mary's Hall.

The primary ghost story centers on ghostly apparitions of men in Whipple Dormitory. They are supposedly crack squad members from school years long ago, standing in the corner of the students' dorm rooms, watching over students to make sure no harm comes to them. But once the student sees them, they vanish into thin air.

Another interesting story at Whipple Hall is of a dog and her puppies. Apparently, the ghost of a female Lab and her puppies has been seen in the hallways, floating three feet above the floor. The reason for them floating that high is because of a fire that burnt the original building down years ago. The floor was three feet higher back then, so the dogs wander around at that level, making one believe they might have perished in the fire. Sometimes you can even feel the dog's wet nose between your legs as you drink from a water fountain within the building.

Other ghostly activity occurs in the theater at the school. Students have seen several ghosts walking on stage late at night as if in a play. They act as if they don't know they're dead.

Overall, there are many reports of objects, such as books and papers, moving around on their own. There is whispering in the hallways of other buildings such as Breck and St. Mary's, but when inspecting to see who the noisy ones are, nobody is there. Some even say they've seen old Headmasters walking down the hallways late at night, as if checking up on the students to make sure no harm has come to them.

Chapter 6
Ellen's Critique

"I don't need any photographs or audiotapes to tell me the place is haunted. I've seen it first hand."

Location: Mantorville

I like to watch a good play now and then, just like everyone else. I even volunteer to help out where I can. But nobody said anything about the ghostly things that went on at the Mantorville Opera House.

I'd just moved to the small town of Mantorville last year and was excited to get involved with the plays at the Opera House. Hanging out behind the scenes doing lights and stage helped bring me back to my years in high school. It was a magical moment for me back then; I loved the bright lights and audience, and the exhilaration of live performances. Apparently that's what Ellen, our ghost, likes too.

It wouldn't be fair to call Ellen a critic, although by her spooky actions around here she's obviously trying to make a point. Her remarks do not come on paper, but through strange occurrences. Sometimes, before a play, a theater prop will go missing, then turn up later in a different spot. Or you'll get cold chills during a performance, possibly a signal from Ellen that she does not approve. Her biggest statements usually come from the lights, which during the last play turned out to be a nightmare.

It started with the stray cat incident. Several high school students who came to see the play were standing out front beforehand, petting a stray cat that wandered by. It wasn't that unusual to have cats stroll by. It was most likely a nearby neighbor's cat.

Suddenly, the door to the theater opened on its own. The stray cat turned toward the door and hissed, with its back arched and hair standing on end—just like the black cats in the movies. The cat then proceeded to run out into the street, which of course is the last place a cat should run. It was hit by a car and flung out across the sidewalk. Still alive, it ran frantically away, down the alley of the theater. After the high school students' initial shock and screams, they searched for the injured cat but could not find it anywhere.

There was no doubt the cat incident had excited Ellen, her ghostly antics started right from the beginning of the show. I could tell this by the way the lighting board had a mind of its own. I was pretty sure it was Ellen, although I've been told other ghosts haunt the place.

A phantom teenage girl has been sighted behind stage in the green room. At first glance, you would have thought she was just an ordinary teenage girl, dressed in a fancy costume for a play. It wasn't like you could see through her, or she was some ghastly demon child. She was ordinary. That was until she vanished. One minute you were there talking and looking at her through a large mirror in the room. But when you turned around to properly address her, she was gone. Vanished.

Then there's the man in the basement. I don't go down there anymore. The last time I did, the lights flickered on and off, with them spending more time off than on. In the darkness I could feel the presence of him. I never saw him, but I knew he was there. Or at least something was there. His favorite place to stay was underneath the steps, so just getting down into the basement was quite the ordeal. You always wondered if he would reach out and grab your ankle on the staircase.

Mysterious occurrences with the lighting system were the most frequent way Ellen communicated with us. She obviously had a lot to say the night of the stray cat incident. The lighting board had a series of sliding switches, each used to dim the lights, or to turn them on and off. Ellen was having fun with the

Mantorville Opera House,
haunted by several different ghosts.

spotlight that night, making it switch from a rocking chair on one side of the stage to a coffin used as a prop on the other side. She particularly liked the coffin, making it virtually impossible to illuminate the rocking chair on cue.

By the end of the play, I had given up, throwing my hands in the air as I watched the lights inside the theater twinkle on and off on their own. Or was it Ellen? Needless to say, the stage manager was not pleased. She looked up at me, angry at my poor choice in lighting, then turned white when she saw my hands in the air while the lights were going wild. The audience didn't notice anything, other than perhaps the lighting was a bit too dramatic or not at all on cue.

The worst part of the night was after the play. Once everything was locked up, I went out to my car. I had this creepy feeling something was wrong. Dead wrong. To this day, I'm not sure why, but I had a feeling that something was underneath my car. I bent down to look, hoping that Ellen, or something worse, didn't jump out at me. As I did so, I saw the eyes of the cat staring back at me. Unfortunately, there was no life left in it. The poor cat had died under my car.

Thoughts of Ellen came to my mind as I wondered if Ellen now had a new cat to play with. A ghost cat. Was Ellen the one that opened the door to the theater, causing the cat to run out and be hit by the car? Possibly.

To this day, my dog does some crazy things when he comes in the theater on weekends to help me cleanup or work on the lighting system. He runs around the place like a wild dog, then suddenly stops and starts barking at an empty corner. Could my dog be chasing the cat that died? Who knows. All I know is that the place is definitely haunted.

There are many other stories I could tell about the Opera House in Mantorville. Others have even seen Ellen, sitting in the front of the theater, staring up at an empty stage as if waiting for the show to start. Still others have heard things up in the balcony, even when nobody is up there. Ellen has been heard walking up and down the stairs behind the stage by the green room, with her large Victorian dress scraping against the side of the narrow staircase as she walked.

Paranormal Investigators have even been here, trying to track down any ghostly activity. They've found several instances where something strange is definitely going on. They have even captured a shadowy figure of Ellen on film, and possibly on audio too. I don't need any photographs or audiotapes to tell me the place is haunted. I've seen it first hand.

History:

The town of Mantorville was founded in 1854. During that time, a general store was built, but later burned down in the early 1900s. Soon after that, the town raised the money to build an opera house. By December of 1918, the Mantorville Opera House was open, showing plays for all to enjoy. The building has been used as a bar, a club, and even City Hall and a Civic Center. The Mantorville Theater Company took over in the 1970s and has been putting on plays ever since.

One interesting fact is that while building the new opera house back in 1918, the architect from Rochester tragically died, being hit by a car while on duty as a traffic cop. Some say his spirit haunts the place, among several others, including Ellen. Perhaps he is the one lurking in the basement, wandering around admiring the architecture he designed, trying to talk to us about how great a building it is.

Ellen is a ghost that was identified back in the 1970s during a Ouija board session. The name came out of the game, but nobody to this day is sure who Ellen is. One picture believed to be Ellen was captured on a couch in the green room backstage. She also likes to hide props for the upcoming plays, making it sometimes difficult for the actors to do their job, not to mention the backstage manager.

One possible theory on the background of Ellen, is that she is a lady from the Victorian era, who had lost her child to influenza. She wanders the opera house now, although perhaps she originally came from when the location was a general store.

Besides Ellen, another ghost haunts the place. At one point during one of the busy seasonal performances, a person working backstage noticed a teenage girl dressed as if she were going on stage. She was all excited about something. Before anyone could talk with her, she disappeared. She could not be found backstage anywhere.

During a recent investigation by a paranormal team, several EVPs were caught on tape. One included a snotty voice saying, 'Move the car! Move the car!' The investigators set a little toy car down in the room, and were asking the spirits to move it, to show that they were there. Apparently the ghost did not like the request. Although it would be interesting to find out if any of the cars parked out in front of the opera house were moved.

The same investigators had a camera mysteriously get unplugged up in the balcony. A motion sensor was setup near the stairway, to capture anything moving. Nobody had walked up there, yet the camera had been unplugged.

Others have also felt the presence of a man in the basement. The impression one gets is that he crouches underneath the staircase, waiting for you to come down. Some have sensed that he is dressed in a harlequin costume. If that's not creepy enough, I don't know what is. Some say a man that used to play piano for the opera house, who died a few years back, may be haunting the place. Perhaps he is the one dressed in costume, roaming the building in search of a piano to play.

One night, someone working there heard a loud clanging sound up in the balcony, like somebody was moving metal chairs around. Not only was there nobody up in the balcony, but there were no chairs up there either.

Lighting seems to be the biggest issue with the ghosts. Numerous times the lights in the opera house go on and off, as if they had a mind of their own. Most of the time the incidents stem from when someone is trying to operate the lighting board during a play. The spotlights and lights on stage may suddenly go dark, or switch on quickly. Lights in the hallway to the bathroom have activity as well, going on and off all on their own.

The stray cat incident was one of the most alarming incidents, with a cat sadly losing its life. The play, a ghost story about a women in black, was being performed at the time, and as described in the story above, a cat gets hit by a car. Afterward the paranormal activity seemed to increase dramatically that night. Most of the activity centered on the lighting system, doing all sorts of changes on its own. Lights on the stage would slowly go up and down, or shut off entirely. It was not too amusing for the stage manager, or the lighting manager who had her hands off the board while watching as the lights did their own thing.

Employees will sometimes bring their pet dogs into the opera house to keep themselves company on the weekend while they work on sets. Many times the dogs will become disturbed, as if something invisible is in the room with them, howling and barking loudly at nothing.

One person working on a weekend in the opera house, painting the walls, became startled as she could feel someone staring at her. Eventually, she couldn't stand it any longer and turned around. Out of the corner of her eye she saw a woman dressed in an old Victorian outfit, sitting in one of the front rows stage right. No sooner had she seen the ghost than it disappeared.

Field Trip:

I have to say that the field trip to the Mantorville Opera House was by far one of the most exciting. With a rich and recent history of paranormal activity, I thought for sure I'd bump into a ghost or two. I wasn't disappointed.

Theatre area of the Mantorville Opera House, showing several possible orbs.

It wasn't like I physically ran into any ghostly spirits, but a couple pictures and some eerie voices on my digital recorder was good enough for me.

I took many pictures while I was there, hoping to find one with a ghoulish figure of some Victorian lady floating across the stage. I didn't find anything like that, but I caught a few classic orb pictures. I'm not a fan of orbs (little balls of energy, presumably an imprint of a ghost flying by). I really don't believe in them, figuring they are just snapshots of dust particles. But I found it odd that in all of my pictures there were not any orbs, or dust if you will. Except one. It had a dozen or so of these tiny little orb creatures. This was in the opera house audience seating area. What was even more odd was that I took several pictures seconds apart from each other. And only one of them had the orbs in it. I would think that if they were tiny dust particles, I'd find them on all the pictures I took in the area. But there was only one of them.

As far as checking for Electronic Voice Phenomena (EVP), I found a few of them. At 7:04 on my last tape, I caught a voice say, 'I don't like that'. It had that snotty girl voice sound, similar to what a paranormal investigation team had caught earlier in the year, when they asked for the spirits to move their toy car.

I captured several other voices, or noises that I can't explain. Keep in mind this was done during the day, so there could be dozens of sounds coming from outside. Inside, however, it was just myself and an employee giving me the tour.

One very interesting voice I heard came when I was in the basement, in the back room. I can hear an EVP at 20:12 on my tape saying, "G'morning Chris'. That made me jump when I later played it back. Nothing like a friendly ghost that knows your name! This was also the room that I received my haunting impression while investigating with the Twin Cities Paranormal Society.

I'm convinced something strange is going on at the Mantorville Opera House. I can't say that I saw any ghosts, but there were plenty of times the hair on my neck stood up.

And a couple of the EVPs made me believe there's more than just plays being performed. So the next time you sit down in the theater to watch one of their incredible performances, take a look around and see if the ghosts are putting on their own show for you, free of charge.

Chapter 7

Gambling Ghost

"I found my boogeyman."

Desolate country road in rural Southeastern Minnesota.

Location: Goodhue County Road 18

Treasure Island Casino is a great place for entertainment—great food, great shows, and great fun. But what I wasn't expecting was the ghostly old man I encountered along Goodhue County Road 18. Makes a guy want to quit gambling.

The casino is located about an hour from the Twin Cities, south beyond Hastings along County Road 18 toward Red Wing. I've gone there many times and really enjoyed myself. Sure, I'll admit I never won much, other than the time I hit a jackpot on the quarter slot machines. That was a night to remember. Except that was also the night I ran into a ghost on the way back home to Bloomington.

I'd been hitting the slot machines for several hours, rotating between nickel and quarter slots. I'm no major gambler, I just like the basic thrill of maybe winning a few thousand dollars. Even a couple hundred bucks would be a nice deal.

That night I finally hit it big. It was nearly 2 A.M. and I was about ready to go home. I here that's usually how it happens. I dropped the quarter in and bingo! Six hundred dollars richer! Quite the excitement indeed.

After a beer and some bragging at the bar, I walked out of the casino to my car. Walking out as a winner felt great, strutting along to my car as if I had just won millions. I was pumped up for the hour-long ride home, but for some reason as soon as I hopped in my car, I was dead tired. I lasted only five minutes on the road before I began doing head bobs, trying desperately to stretch my eyes open and stay awake. Even with all the windows down and loud rock music blaring away, I couldn't keep the eyes open.

I knew it was dangerous to be driving like that. I had a friend in high school that totaled his car by falling asleep at the wheel. Thankfully, he got out of it without hardly a scratch. I'd heard of others that were not so lucky. I did not want to be one of those unlucky ones.

After crossing the Vermillion River, I decided to pull over and take a short nap. Thirty minutes of sleep would do the trick, allowing me to make it the rest of the way home. I've done that many times before; a little catnap rejuvenated me every time. There was a spot to park well off the road. I pulled over far enough as to not be disturbed, or be bothered by a policeman driving by.

I took the keys out of the ignition and put them in the glove compartment. Someone once told me to do that if you pull over and sleep, and if you've had a couple beers. I'd only had three beers the whole night, so I knew I wasn't drunk. But I wasn't going to take any chances either. With my driver's side seat reclined, I rolled on my side facing the side window and closed my eyes. No sooner had I done so when I heard a strange shuffling noise outside.

It sounded like somebody was dragging something on the ground, something heavy. The sound was getting louder too. It was definitely getting closer whatever it was. I could tell it was footsteps, with one foot stepping and then the other being dragged, as if somebody was trying to walk with a broken leg.

I hadn't opened my eyes yet, and because I was starting to get spooked, I didn't want to. Too many horror movies I suppose. But I really didn't want to open my eyes and find some ghostly phantom staring at me from the driver's side window.

The stepping and shuffling got louder, then stopped. Next it felt like my car shifted a little, like somebody had just leaned up against it. It also got cold. Real cold. The only problem was that it was the middle of July, and at least seventy degrees out. There was no logical explanation for my sudden chills, and I didn't want to believe some paranormal activity was occurring. I didn't believe in ghosts. At least not until that night.

They say curiosity killed the cat, but I think it can also scare the pants off it too, if a cat could wear pants that is. After a minute of sitting there pretending to sleep with my eyes shut tight, I got up the nerve to open my eyes. I did a quick blink, opening them briefly, then shutting them again. Afterwards I realized that was probably more stupid than leaving them open. If I did see some ghoulish figure staring at me with beady red eyes, I don't think closing my eyes would have helped. I'd just end up having to open them again, being freaked out a second time.

I was safe. There was nothing showing up out my window. I chuckled a moment, thinking of how childish I was, getting scared of the boogeyman. I wasn't anywhere near a closet, right? Well, my chuckles turned to gagging as I rolled over to face my passenger's side window. I found my boogeyman.

People talk about being so scared they can't move. Total paralysis. I can now say I've lived through that experience. I'm just glad my heart didn't stop (although I think it did, but thankfully started beating again). I stared at this person; he was an old man, with seriously wrinkled skin, and ghostly white and black hair streaking back as if he'd been electrocuted. I knew the nuclear power plant was nearby. Perhaps he was an employee that got zapped and floated down river? Then I noticed his eyes, or the lack of them. Where his eyes should be, I only saw darkness, except for the red pupils staring at me.

When he started tapping on the window I snapped out of my trance. My first thought was to get the heck out of there. Unfortunately, I had to reach out near him into the glove compartment and get my keys. What a dumb idea that was, stashing them in there. Visions flickered through my mind of the ghoulish old man smashing the window and biting my arm off as I attempted to retrieve my keys.

He saw me reaching for the glove compartment, and for some reason that made him tap faster. Harder too. I thought for sure he would break through the window any second. Luckily, I was able to get my keys out easily. Unfortunately, they slipped from my fingers and dropped to the floor of the passenger's side.

This is where I wish I had a car like Fred Flintstone. No keys needed. Just put the feet to the ground and start moving. Of course, I imagine the phantom old man would be crawling up through the floor then. Or maybe some futuristic car that you commanded to go. Although I was too petrified to even yell. Trying to command my car to drive away would no doubt send me into the river.

As I spent the next minute bobbing into the passenger side floor, trying to get my keys and not spend too much time near the ghost, I realized it had gone. I breathed a sigh of relief as I finally reached down and picked up my keys. Of course, I already had the feeling that it wasn't gone completely. The hair standing straight up on my neck was a dead give away. I figured it was most likely on my side of the car now. I was right.

Now I spent the next minute leaning way, far away from the driver's side window, the whole time trying to fit the key into the ignition with my fumbling fingers. It's truly amazing how inept one can become in the face of fear. I was what you would call an extreme bumbling idiot. If there were a competition for ineptitude, I would have easily won.

For some reason I found myself staring at the ghoulish old man, and I could tell he was smiling. Laughing too, with a big toothless grin, like this was some big joke. It was no laughing matter to me. I wasn't sure what it would do to me if it got in the car. Finally, I got the key in the ignition. It started up right away. I was thankful for that. Especially since the ghost was now pounding hard on my window. I thought at any moment it would shatter. It was my turn to smile now. I shifted into reverse, backing up while kicking gravel into the air. I put my car into drive and blew out of there. I watched in my rearview mirror, half expecting the ghostly old man to be following me, but he didn't. I was able to make it home without any further incident. And I wasn't sleepy either.

I still go to the casino, and still have loads of fun. But I don't stay late any more. Or if I do, I get a hotel room. But I close the curtains when I'm there. I don't know, I just feel better knowing I won't wake up in the middle of the night with some ghostly old man staring back at me through the window.

History:

The drive to the casino takes you through some rural areas and at night, this alone can make you feel quite creepy. If not from the fear of bumping into a ghost, you would at least be fearful of hitting a deer as it crossed the road.

Having lived near the area, I've traveled the road a few times. I even made it to the casino once. Lots of fun. And no, I didn't walk away with any jackpot winnings. I've also traveled on the road to tour the nuclear power plant nearby. The casino was built on a Native American Reservation not too far from Red Wing. With that in mind, one would think there would be many Native American ghost stories. Still, the area was very busy back in the 1800s, with many towns springing up out of nowhere to help the logging industry. Perhaps the ghostly man on the road is an old logger, tragically dying from a logging accident in the late 1800s. The whole area along the Mississippi

River is teaming with history of Native Americans, fur traders, and logging men.

The paranormal activity described in the area (there have been several sightings of this) is of an old man in rags hobbling along the road. He comes up to your parked car, rapping on the window. At this point, whoever is in the car immediately leaves. Other reports have indicated that a slow-walking man can be found hobbling along the road late at night, although nobody's sure if it's the same man. I doubt very many would stop to find out.

There was one other report of a man and woman picking up hitchhikers after leaving the casino. As it turns out, they did not pick anyone up at all. The woman in the car noticed nobody was in the back seat. But they both could sense something was there. The man driving appeared to have fallen into a trance, driving along as if people were in fact in the back seat. After awhile the woman wised up and shook off the eerie feeling. She demanded the man stop the car. At that point, the woman opened the car door and immediately told whatever was in the back seat to leave. Some dark shadowy presence floated out of the car, at which time the couple took off, never to return.

Having lived in rural Minnesota most of my life, I can tell you firsthand the roads late at night can make you feel creepy. There are many desolate roads in Southeast Minnesota, all of which you find yourself staring toward the side of the road for deer, and perhaps the occasional ghost. Of course, running into a ghost does much less damage on your car than a deer. I've yet to hear someone claim they hit a ghost and their car was totaled.

So be careful traveling back from the casino, especially if you've lost a few bucks. And if you won a jackpot, watch out for the phantom tax collector—he may take more than just your money.

Chapter 8
Ghost at the Y

"I'm still not entirely sure what we saw, but I know it wasn't human-or at least not anymore."

YMCA building in Winona, reported to be haunted by the ghost of a janitor.

Location: Winona

Swimming can be a great activity on a Friday night, or any other time of the week. But when you end up diving into a pool full of ghosts, well, that's not at all a fun thing to do...

Okay, it wasn't exactly a pool full of ghosts. It was just one ghost. Supposedly, it's the janitor who used to work at the YMCA in Winona. I'm told he's a friendly ghost, wanting to make sure everything is clean and safe. Friendly or not, ghosts are still creepy. If I had a choice I'd stay far away from them. But I guess it wasn't my choice Friday night at the Y.

My son Jake and I go to the YMCA in Winona all the time. Never had any issues, other than having the water temperature a little cold sometimes. And we never saw any ghosts or spooky things like that. Actually, I'm still not entirely sure what we saw, but I know it wasn't human—or at least not anymore.

I was surprised to see there weren't that many people swimming. We usually came on Saturday and it was always packed full of kids splashing and doing huge cannon ball dives. The fun thing then was to see how many adults you could get wet who were sitting in patio chairs along the side. I knew better and always made sure I was wearing a swimsuit while watching from the chairs. Unfortunately, the dad next to me last Saturday wasn't so lucky.

A rather large kid jumped in and created the biggest cannon ball wave I've ever seen. A huge volume of water leaped out of the pool and slapped the dad across his chest while he sat there trying to read the newspaper. Needless to say, the newspaper did not make it, and the dad was not at all amused.

Friday night there wasn't anybody in the pool area. Just Jake and I. That was fine with me. A little father-son quality time would be great. What I didn't expect was the tapping on the pool area door. A little tapping would have been fine, and if a person would have come in, even better. Instead, I eventually got out of the pool and opened the door. Nobody was there.

After several of these tapping incidents, I became annoyed. Since Jake had to take a bathroom break, he went into the locker room while I quickly darted down to the front desk to complain.

"I don't want to bother you too much, but someone keeps tapping on the pool door entrance, then runs away. Every time I go over to let them in, nobody's there."

The girl at the front desk, young, perhaps about seventeen, turned white.

"What's the matter?" I asked.

"Quit making fun of her," said a teenage boy, Scott, from the other side of the front desk.

"What do you mean?"

"It's the ghost," replied Scott. "You're teasing her about the janitor ghost. Look, there's no such thing as ghosts."

I looked at the boy, not clear what he was saying. "I don't know what you're talking about. Look, all I know is that somebody is annoying me and I'd like you to look into it."

Scott looked at Julie, then said, "Sure. I can check it out."

The two of us walked back down the hallway toward the pool area. I hadn't heard about any ghosts at the Y, and hadn't thought about ghosts in general for years. Not since high school when we use to play around with Tarot cards and Ouija boards.

"Sorry for startling the girl," I said to Scott.

"No problem. She's just a little wound up lately, ever since last week when she came face to face with the ghost."

"I don't believe in ghosts," I quickly added.

"Me neither," said Scott with a smile, then added, "but since I started working here, I've begun to change my mind."

"Really," was I all could say, intrigued by his statement. I looked at his face and could tell he was sincere. Trying not to chuckle I said, "What sort of ghost do you have?"

"He's a janitor. Used to work here. He's a cool ghost, friendly. Some say he's saved a few lives around here, kids almost drowning in the pool, or weightlifters slipping with weights while doing massive bench presses."

"Interesting," I said, which was true. Although I was more fascinated with Scott in seeing how he truly believed in what he was saying.

A garbage can rattled in the hallway just ahead of us. It then turned over, rolling back and forth as if somebody was playing with it.

Scott pointed ahead and nervously smiled. "There he is. The janitor. He does that a lot."

I was beginning to get spooked out myself. Furthermore, Jake was certainly done using the bathroom by now and would be looking for me by the poolside. I was confident he wouldn't be swimming. He knew better than to do that without me.

We reached the spot where the trashcan tipped over. Scott picked it up and set it back where it was. He tapped on the top and said, "Thanks, Mr. Janitor. We know you're here to help."

I was a little uncomfortable with how comfortable the boy was in dealing with the ghost, and how it had mysteriously tipped over the cans. Of course, I wasn't entirely convinced it was a ghost. That was until I felt it brush against my body.

It's somewhat hard to explain. The feeling was basically like someone just hit you with a blast of super-cooled air. Maybe it's how you feel when you open the freezer and stick your head inside. Not a good feeling if you ask me.

Scott laughed. "Hey! He likes you! Bumps into people he likes. It's his way of saying hi."

I was not finding it amusing at all. Every bone in my body felt as if it had just been dumped into a deep freeze. Thankfully, the feeling only lasted a few seconds.

We reached the door to the pool area and the boy just stood there, tapping on it a few times.

"Did it sound something like that?" he asked.

"Yes, exactly like that."

"Well, I can't do much about it right now. I'll wait by the door and watch for awhile." He smiled and said, "Maybe I'll bump into the janitor."

I'd had enough of the janitor ghost stuff and wanted to get back to Jake. I nodded to the boy and turned to go into the pool. What I found inside sent shivers through my body.

There was Jake, floating in the deeper end, well above his head, smiling and splashing away. The only problem was that Jake didn't know how to swim yet. There was no logical explanation as to how he could have been afloat.

"Jake!" I yelled while running through the pool area to him. "Don't worry, I'll get you!"

"What do you mean?" he asked, happily floating and playing in the water.

I dove into the pool, swimming rapidly over to him. As I got closer, I could have sworn I saw something in the water, underneath him, holding him up. Someone wearing a blue shirt and jeans. *Could it be the janitor?* I thought momentarily. *Impossible.* I reached around Jake, pulling him in near me. "Are you okay?"

Jake laughed and said, "Yeah, sure."

"But you're swimming in the deep end, over your head."

He looked around and said, "Yeah, I guess so. But a man was here and helped me." Jake laughed and added, "And he went swimming with his clothes on!"

I was more terrified then ever. Had the janitor ghost come rushing past me in the hallway, diving into the pool to save my son? *Impossible.* Still, I couldn't explain what had happened. With the excitement at hand, I was done swimming. We hopped out of the pool and walked past Scott, who was still waiting on the other side of the door.

"Look," said Scott, pointing down to the floor. Wet footprints led from the pool area down the hallway. "I bet they go right to the janitor's closet," he said with a smile.

I'd definitely had enough. Jake and I showered up and went home. We don't go to the Y on Friday nights anymore. We stick to Saturdays, and when it's really busy. Don't get me wrong. I'm very appreciative of the janitor ghost. If it wasn't for him, my son would probably not be alive today.

History:

In the case of this ghost story, all activity centers on the idea that a janitor still haunts the building. It was difficult to find a lot of evidence on the ghostly activity. My thought is that the story is just that, a story.

Still, employees have mentioned that it is common to hear mop buckets and brooms bumping around in the closet, falling to the ground late at night. Objects in the building mysteriously move around, and doors will open and close on their own. Occasionally, a whispering voice can be heard as well.

To add to the story, apparently the lights went out in the building when the funeral procession for the janitor drove by outside. It was later assumed a squirrel had caused the outage, but who's to say the janitor didn't chase the squirrel into the transformer?

Other employees deny any such paranormal activity. They add that it's a great ghost story, but there's never been anything paranormal going on in the building. Perhaps the story about the ghostly janitor is that, just a story. Either way, I think the next time you visit your local YMCA to go swimming, don't be alarmed if the lifeguard isn't there. A ghostly janitor will be there to help you.

Chapter 9

Haunting at the Hubbell

"Chills ran through my body as I pictured the dead man walking around the place, as if he didn't know he was dead."

The famous Hubbell House of Mantorville, visited by many guests, including the ghost of Mr. Hubbell himself.

Location: Mantorville

'd already had my lunch at the Hubbell House. Excellent food. Now it was time to get to work. Ghost hunting to be exact.

It was nice to sneak into a place without anybody knowing you're here to look for ghosts. Nobody knew that my digital audio recorder would soon be flying about the place, searching for the proverbial electronic voice phenomena, EVP for short.

Usually when you come into a place and introduce yourself as a ghost hunter, their eyes immediately widen, as if they thought you were a ghost. Sometimes I want to yell, 'Boo!', but I know that would be unprofessional. Although the ghosts I hunt aren't very professional. They either scare the heck out of you, or don't show up at all.

At the Hubbell House I had decided to go incognito at first, sitting down and enjoying the great ambience with a relaxing bacon cheeseburger and glass of iced tea. I'd normally have a refreshing Schell's beer on tap, but not when ghost hunting. The last thing I wanted was to be tipsy in front of a full-bodied apparition. Worse yet, being intoxicated while investigating can easily make you miss some obvious activity, or sometimes make you think you see things.

With my meal finished and paid, I decided to let the waitress know who I was. As soon as I said my name, the eyes widened. Just like always. I refrained from saying, 'Boo!', barely. She smiled and promptly walked over to the bartender. He was the one I wanted to interview. He's the one that all this stuff was happening to.

As the waitress told the bartender my name, I waited for his eyes to widen, but they didn't. He casually looked at me and nodded. That alarmed me. It usually meant the guy was real; he'd seen a ghost or two and wasn't spooked by it. He waved me over to the bar.

"Care for a drink?" he asked.

I shook my head and with a smile said, "No, not while I'm working."

He stared at me as if trying to figure out if I made a joke or not. Then he glanced over my shoulder to his right. Instinctively, I looked too, but saw nothing other than a door leading into another room. Trying to cut the tension I jokingly said, "Did you see a ghost?"

Pausing a moment, still looking at the door he replied, "Yes. I believe I did."

The bar area had several patrons still eating, but none of them noticed anything odd. I didn't see anything either as I looked around, but apparently the bartender did.

"What did it look like?" I asked.

Ignoring my question, he nodded toward the back room and said, "Back there. That's where Mr. Hubbell stays. See him there all the time, smoking cigars and hanging out."

At first I thought he was joking. But I could tell by the look in his eyes that he was serious. I brought out my digital audio recorder and asked, "Mind if I record our chat?"

Nodding, he said, "And check for EVPs I presume."

He knew his ghosts. I nodded and clicked the recorder, which then emitted a small L.E.D. light on the front of it. The digital recorder was my lifeblood. It not only captured all the information about the stories, but also the occasional EVP.

The bartender proceeded to tell me about the ghost of Mr. Hubbell. How he had been seen walking through the bar area, floating more than anything. Always heading to the back room. The bartender explained how the room was one of the original rooms from back in the late 1800s, and that Mr. Hubble liked to smoke a few cigars now and then. As he was saying this, I swear I could smell cigar smoke, coming from the back room. I could tell the bartender smelled it too. Since the place had been smoke-free for years, it was definitely a peculiar incident.

"I'd take you in the back room, but I'm working the bar right now."

"That's fine," I said. I was really here now just to do the interview. If everything checked out, and there were some real stories, I'd notified a local group of paranormal investigators to come out and verify the hauntings. I've found over the years that most stories are just that, stories. They're based on perhaps a fragment of paranormal activity. Most of the work investigating is done disproving stories. "Anything else odd happen around here? How about the guy in the basement?"

The bartender smiled and said, "You mean the guy that hung himself down there?"

His smile alarmed me. For him to be so callous at first, smiling with a wide grin about somebody who died one floor below, well, that made me shiver more than the ghosts do.

"There was an employee, a maintenance man I believe, who worked here years ago. I don't recall his name. Guess that doesn't matter. What does matter is that he hung himself in the basement."

He paused, looking at my expression. Perhaps he was trying to read my face, looking for my eyes to get wide. I don't get spooked by stories. Not that easily anyway. But this one sure tested me.

"What happened to him?" I asked.

"Well, after he hung himself, we kept seeing him walking around here, like nothing ever happened."

That was confusing. How could he have hung himself, then still be walking around? The bartender could tell I was perplexed.

"His ghost. The ghost of the maintenance man was up here walking around. For several days. I wasn't here at the time, but I've talked to a waitress that was. She said you wouldn't have known he was dead. He looked real, walking around like nothing had happened."

"How do you know he was already dead? He could have been walking around alive, then killed himself later."

"That's what we thought at first. But you could tell his body was down there for a couple days. The autopsy proved it as well."

Chills ran through my body as I pictured the dead man walking around the place, as if he didn't know he was dead. Like he had some plumbing to fix, or light bulbs to change. I wondered for a moment if that's what it was like after we die. Do we just continue to walk this earth, never really knowing that we are no more? More chills hit me, but this time it felt like it came from an external source.

Usually I don't get spooked by stories, but this one turned my stomach inside out. I started getting the feeling that the ghostly maintenance man was standing right behind me, hovering over my right shoulder as if waiting for me to give him a maintenance request. Instinctively, I turned to look and jumped back in my chair, almost falling out.

The waitress was there and said, "Here's your change."

Out of the corner of my eye I thought I saw something move, heading to the back room. I looked to see the door swing shut. Did Mr. Hubbell just walk in? Or was it the maintenance man going to fix a light bulb? A rush of cold air blew past me, with a hint of cigar smoke in it.

That was enough for me. I'd seen a few weird things while investigating haunted places. I'll admit I'm sort of a skeptic. But with this place I was beginning to believe. What concerned me more was how spooky I felt. This was the middle of the day. It wasn't like I was in the back room of some basement during the witching hour. Or a moonlit cemetery with the wind howling and owls hooting from a nearby tree. Lots of people were around, none of them seemed scared. The hair on my arms began to rise. Something was here alright. But not me. It was time for me to leave. Something didn't feel right. "Keep the change," I said to the waitress as I stumbled out of my chair, my face was probably white as ghost.

The bartender could tell I was spooked. He smiled and waved at me, no doubt enjoying the look on my face. "Come back again sometime. Maybe I can introduce you to Mr. Hubbell. And the maintenance man is always wandering around, looking for things to fix."

History:

First and foremost, the Hubble House is an incredible place to visit with friends and family, and to have an excellent meal. Besides having great food, the building itself is a beautiful opportunity to experience early American hospitality.

During the move west of the Mississippi back in the 1800s, many wagons pushed through La Crosse on their way to the

Great Plains. The area around Mantorville became an early stopping point along one's journey. Shortly after Minnesota became a state, Frank Mantor declared Mantorville a town. John Hubbell soon constructed the Hubbell House for travelers coming through who needed a good place to relax and eat.

It was originally a 16 foot by 24 foot log structure, but by 1856 (two years later), they built the current three-story structure. It quickly became a frequent stop for those traveling from the Mississippi to St. Peter. Over the years, many guests have stayed or visited the Hubbell House, including Senator Ramsey, General U.S. Grant, Bishop Whipple, and Dr. W.W. Mayo.

As far as ghostly encounters at the historic Hubbell House, many things have occurred. Things have been known to become misplaced, or have been mysteriously moved around. Drinking glasses will slide across the bar on their own, or chairs will have been moved around in the middle of the night, even though nobody was there.

In other situations, lights will be turned on (and off) without anyone being around. Numerous times, employees will find the rooms with lights on, especially the light in the basement. More peculiar is how bulbs will mysteriously burn out, needing to be replaced more frequently than usual. Perhaps the maintenance man is making work for himself to do, or having trouble trying to change light bulbs now that he is a ghost.

One of the most common paranormal happenings is with Mr. Hubbell himself. The bartender, among others, have seen him walking through the bar area dressed in formal early 1900s clothing. He glides across the room, headed for the old part of the house into a back room. He doesn't interact with anyone, seeming too intent on getting to the back room. Perhaps that's a place of comfort for him, a relaxing area for him to sit down and smoke a good cigar. The smell of cigar smoke can still be found lingering in the bar area, even though nobody has smoked cigars in the place for years.

Another eerie incident at the Hubbell House deals with the unfortunate event of an employee who sadly died in the basement. No one knows why, but one night he hung himself from the rafters in the basement. What's mysterious about this is that he had not been found for several days, yet everyone noticed him walking around, after he was dead. Some say he wandered around the Hubbell House, still wanting to work there and fix things up. It was a place he loved to be in, which makes sense as to why he would still want to be there, even after he had died.

Field Trip:

While doing my investigation of the Mantorville Opera House, I had a chance to eat lunch there and discuss the opera house. During that time, I had my digital recorder going to take notes. I also hoped to possibly find some EVPs at the Hubbell House. Unfortunately, it was a bit too noisy in the room for me to pickup anything. Fortunately, the food was excellent. I recommend the bacon cheeseburger and iced tea.

At the time of this writing, I did not have an opportunity to do a real investigation of the building. Twin Cities Paranormal Society (www.twincitiesparanormalsociety.com), however, were planning to do so, but I have not yet heard their results at the time of this writing. I'm sure they will find some interesting things there. The Hubbell House is definitely a place to visit. Great food and great ghosts. What else is there?

Chapter 10
Haunting Heffron Hall

"Little did I know what was waiting in my dorm room."

Sketch of Heffron Hall at St. Mary's College, where students and staff have reported many strange paranormal events.

Location: Winona

I was shocked to hear about the ghost of Heffron Hall at St. Mary's College. As a freshman, I'd been living in the men's dorm on the third floor for several months and never had any terrifying experiences. That is until recently.

Apparently, it has been a college tradition to have the upper classmen tell stories about the ghosts. They'd coral the freshmen into a room on the third floor of Heffron Hall, light a few candles, put on some spooky music, and tell stories about the horrors that have happened. About Father Lesches' attempt to murder Bishop Heffron, back in the early 1900s during the consecration of the Holy Eucharist, and how Lesches haunts the halls today.

The mysterious fiery death of Father Lynch was weaved into the story, along with a student dying every eight years, and of course this was the eighth year (it was always the eighth year). Ghostly events and spooky stories never interested me that much. I guess I out grew them. But no amount of growing can take me away from the terror I experienced last month in my dorm room.

It was early November with the air outside cold and dry. I could see frosty dew forming on the grass in front of Heffron Hall as I walked back from a late night at the library. My watch showed 11:30 A.M.; I had been studying for several hours, and unfortunately had more to do up in my room. With two mid-term tests in the morning, there was no time for fun—or probably sleep. If I were lucky I'd get my test cramming done by 3 or 4 A.M., then get a couple hours of rest. Little did I know what was waiting for me in my dorm room.

Everything appeared to be normal at first. My roommate was gone, out partying no doubt. He didn't take the studying and grades too serious. Most likely he would become one of the freshmen statistics, not making it past the first semester. I, on the other hand, wanted to get through and knew I had to work hard to do it. Studying was a way of life for me, I just wished I could have studied in peace that night. Of course, the ghost of Heffron Hall had other ideas.

I was able to study for about an hour, until 1 A.M. in the morning. That's when something odd happened. The light on my ceiling began to flicker, like a bulb going bad. It wasn't spooky or anything like that, although the stories from the upper classmen did make me briefly wonder. But then my door opened. I thought it odd for this to happen, especially since I knew it was locked. The light in my room got dimmer as I stared at the door, waiting for perhaps my roommate to come staggering in, reeking of beer or kamikaze on his breath, depending on what the party flavor of the night was. But nothing came in, except what I thought was a shadowy figure.

The dark figure hovered near the door for a few seconds, then darted back out, slamming the door behind it. That got my attention. As I said, I didn't believe in any of the paranormal stuff. But having my locked door open up on its own and see this shadowy figure, well, it gave me the creeps. I walked over to check my door. It was still locked. *Too much studying,* I thought. *Need to get some sleep.* I shrugged the strange incident off, thinking it was my mind playing tricks on me, and continued my late night studying.

At about 1:30 A.M., I heard this tapping sound outside my door in the hallway. It was as if somebody were rapping a metal cane on the tile floor. Normally at this time of night there would be some noises from students coming back from the bars. But with most others studying all evening for their own midterm tests, not too many were out partying. Most were in their dorms either sleeping or studying like me.

The tapping on the floor was getting louder, and more annoying in my opinion. It was making it difficult for me to study. Finally, I ran to the door and threw it open, just when I thought the tapping noise was right outside my room. The tapping stopped, but there was nobody there.

I saw Carl, another freshman coming out of the bathroom. "Did you hear any tapping?" I asked.

He looked at me confused. "Tapping? No. I didn't hear anything from the bathroom." Carl walked down the opposite way through the hallway and into his dorm room.

I turned around to go back in my room, when suddenly a rush of cold chilling air blew by me, hitting the billboard across the hall and rustling the papers stapled to it. First of all, I've had some cold winds blow by me in Minnesota, but this was frigid. Frosted up my breath even. It only lasted a few seconds, but that was enough to make me go in and put on a jacket.

Needless to say, my continued studying did not go well. I was too spooked by the recent activity. I still didn't think they were ghost related, but then I couldn't come up with any other plausible explanations. I settled in to my desk for another hour of studying. That would be enough to get me through the tests in the morning.

By 2:15 A.M., I was done. Not because of any ghostly incidents, but because I was too tired to study anymore. My eyelids were more closed than open. Shuffling off to the bathroom for a pit stop before bed, I couldn't help but to think about the ghost of Heffron Hall. Supposedly, most of its activity was between 1 A.M. and 3 A.M. In the many times I've been up studying late, I've never seen anything that weird. But when I went to wash my hands, a thick, dark-red liquid came out; I freaked out.

Blood? I thought to myself as I backed up. *No way. It can't be.* I shook my head and looked again. This time it was just plain water. I washed my hands in it and could tell it was normal H_2O. But just to be safe, I skipped brushing my teeth that night.

I was sure that too much studying and not enough sleep was the cause of my hallucinations. For finals I would make sure I got plenty of sleep. I left my sweatpants on to sleep in, since it was unusually cold in the dorm. Part of me deep down was glad I wore them, just in case I had to leave in the middle of the night. Say for instance, if a ghost tried to strangle me. Of course, that's exactly what happened.

I fell asleep quickly, but it was a fitful one, compressed with many not so nice dreams and eerie feelings. Then I woke up (or at least I thought I woke up) to find this shadowy figure had crept into the room, right through the door. It hovered at the foot of my bed, watching me. I couldn't tell what kind of face it had; it was all black and sort of see-through. Suddenly, I felt like I couldn't breathe. The figure was gone from the foot of my bed, and standing (or hovering) beside me.

Its arms, or whatever it had for appendages, reached forth around my neck, constricting my breathing, which was quite rapid at this point. And there was that feeling. The feeling of death. Everything felt dark and disturbing, like there was a tremendous amount of pressure in the room, not just on my neck. I guess I would say it felt like evil, some unholy ghost of a thing trying to suffocate me.

I started to feel like I was going to black out. Of course, if I was dreaming, no big deal, right? Well, dreaming or not, I was petrified. I figured I'd either die of asphyxiation or a heart attack. The shadowy figure really terrified me. I'd never felt that scared in my life.

Not sure of what to do, I put my own hands up around my neck. The area around my neck was cold, making my hands go numb. I wrestled a moment with this shadow figure, trying desperately to remove its hands from my neck. Then, in an instant it was over. The black shadow thing was gone, and I was awake, struggling with my bed sheet that had been twisted and wrapped around my neck.

Looking at the clock I saw that it was 2:45 A.M. and I was soaked. The nightmare (or reality—to this day I'm still not sure), had caused me to break out in a serious sweat, or a terrible bedwetting. Looking around the room, I could sense something was still not right. I had that feeling, as if somebody was still watching me. I turned my reading light on by my bed, giving me a chance to look. I wished I hadn't done that.

Hovering right above me was a white, translucent apparition. A ghost. It didn't look all gross or ghastly, just a regular face of a middle-aged man. But it didn't look happy. If anything it seemed mad or angry. Instinctively, I swung at the face. I nearly broke every bone in my hand. This thing was real.

That was enough for me. In ghost stories they always describe how your hands go right through the ghost's body. Not true. At least for me. I was sure my hand was broken. But I wasn't going to stay there and check it out. I was out of there. Grabbing my jacket and shoes I ran out the door. I'd be spending the rest of the night in my car, parked a long way from Heffron Hall. Perhaps across the Mississippi in Wisconsin.

They say you should never look back when you're running away from ghosts. I guess I wasn't smart enough to pay attention to that rule. Because when I got to the end of the hallway, stopping only to put my shoes and jacket on, I felt like something was running after me. I didn't see anything, but I felt it. Before I knew it, I was smacked hard in the shoulder and dropped to the floor.

I lay there awhile, trying to shove my shoes on, wondering what other invisible things would terrorize me. Thankfully, the ghost of Heffron Hall was done. It was 3:01 A.M. I raced down the stairs to my car, fumbling with the keys due to my surely broken hand. I dropped the keys several times while trying to start the car, each time wondering if I'd sit back up and see that face again in the reflection of my car window.

I made it to Wisconsin. Sleeping in my car was much better, parked in front of a Super America. You may ask about the midterm tests the next day? Well, I didn't take them. Never went back to the dorm. Never finished college either. All because of the ghost of Heffron Hall (at least that's my excuse).

History:

St. Mary's College has been around since 1912, when Bishop Heffron, the second bishop of the Winona Diocese, decided to provide higher education for the young men of Southern Minnesota. It originally started as an academy and junior college, but by 1925 became a four-year liberal arts college.

As far as ghost stories go, the ghost of Heffron Hall is one of the most famous in Minnesota. Ever since the *Nexus*, the local newspaper of St. Mary's College, printed the story, everyone seems to know about it. Even *USA Today* has published a story on the haunting ghost, noting St. Mary's College as one of the most legendary haunted places.

The background for this story is that a priest, Father Lesches, attempted to assassinate Bishop Heffron on the morning of August 27, 1915. Father Lesches entered the chapel on the second floor of St. Mary's Hall with a gun. Just after Bishop Heffron consecrated the Host, Father Lesches fired three shots. One missed, the other hit Bishop Heffron in the leg. The third shot missed but hit the Tabernacle. A fourth shot was fired point blank, narrowly missing his heart.

Bishop Heffron survived the ordeal, Father Lesches was later arrested by the Winona Police. Father Lesches was found to be insane and committed to the State Hospital for the Dangerously Insane in St. Peter, Minnesota. He died in the asylum on January 10, 1943 between 1:30 and 2:00 A.M. But that didn't stop more problems from occurring.

While Father Lesches was in the asylum, Father Lynch who was still at St. Mary's College, mysteriously died the night of May 14, 1931. A malfunctioning reading lamp was supposedly the cause, electrocuting him in his bed. Rumors spread that Father Lesches was the cause, even though he was locked up in the asylum over a hundred miles away. There have been reports that Father Lynch's body was severely burned, charred from the electrocuting lamp. No one can explain how a small reading lamp could cause that much burning over his whole body. What's even more mysterious is that nothing of his bed burned.

To this day, it has been assumed that Father Lesches is haunting Heffron Hall at St. Mary's. And many students have experienced paranormal activity. One student claims to have had an incident in the bathroom, where a sickening, thick, fluid came out of the sink faucet, similar to blood.

Other eerie reports are of the cold spots traveling up and down the hallway, along with a phantom mist. It's also been said that you can hear the tapping of Father Lesches brass cane out in the hallway, and that a student dies every eight years on campus. According to records, Father Lesches did have a cane. But students are not dying every eight years.

It's one thing to play with college ghost stories, to get your blood pumping late at night. But it's another thing to experience real ghosts. Several students on campus claim to have seen dark shadowy figures moving about. One such student clearly remembers back in October of 2001 around 1:30 A.M., a dark presence at the edge of her bed while she was just about falling asleep. She suddenly felt like she was being suffocated. Eventually, the feeling went away. At first, she shrugged off the idea that it was some ghostly presence. That is until she found out another girl down the hall had the exact same experience that night.

In 2002, another student became terrified as he watched the door to his dorm room open and close by itself. A shadowy figure came into the room. The blinds on the window were closed, so there was no possible way a shadow was coming in from the outside. Then suddenly the shadow moved away, and the door slammed shut. Others have bumped into this shadowy figure, including some faculty.

Along with the dark figure, third floor Heffron Hall's furniture tended to get rearranged, and electrical equipment behaved strangely. TVs would go on and off, and CD players would skip songs or replay them at will. It was most common late at night between 1 and 3 A.M., the time when Father Lesches died at the State Hospital of the Criminally Insane.

Another student ended up staying in Heffron Hall a few days before any of the other students one fall. She woke up one night to the sound of smoke alarms randomly going off. Then her alarm clock began going off. The only problem was that it wasn't plugged in and there weren't any batteries in it. Needless to say, she left the dorm right away.

With as much analysis and investigation that has been done, many believe the whole ordeal could be the making of a great prank, originally put forth by *Nexus*, the local college newspaper back in the late 1960s. Still, others believe something paranormal is going on there, for they have had firsthand experiences. It makes one wonder which came first, the story or the ghost? In the case of the ghost of Heffron Hall, perhaps it was the story first, then the ghost. Either way, I'd be careful sleeping on the third floor of Heffron Hall. And if you hear tapping outside your door, be careful opening it. It may just be the ghost of Father Lesches, looking for his final revenge.

Chapter 11
A Night with TCPS

"By the pricking of my thumbs, something wicked this way comes..."
—William Shakespeare in Macbeth

Restoration House in Mantorville, one of several places visited by Twin Cities Paranormal Society during their Paranormal Investigation.

Location: Mantorville

I thought I'd add this chapter in about the experiences I had going out on the town with a real ghost hunting crew, the Twin Cities Paranormal Society. They were lined up to visit the town of Mantorville. All of the town. Yep, they had numerous sites setup to investigate around the area.

For those of you who have not visited Mantorville, I suggest you do. Not only for the spooky locations in various buildings, but for the wonderful, heart-warming experience of the cozy town nestled along the Root River. Besides hiking and biking on the nearby trails, you can stop in for a delicious bite to eat at the historic Hubble House. And if you're dining late into the evening, why not stop by the Opera House for a local play, put on by the Mantorville Theater Company. Perhaps you'll even see a ghost or two.

The Twin Cities Paranormal Society came down from the Cities for the weekend to investigate several locations and were gracious enough to let me tag along—and even help out on a few investigations.

Just prior to the investigation starting, the Mantorville Theater Company put on a play that showed at 8 P.M. I couldn't resist the opportunity to watch an excellent theatrical performance, and perhaps be visited by a ghost or two during the play, since the building was seriously haunted.

The play was spectacular to watch, I enjoyed it thoroughly. I did find myself veering off to the different corners of the theatre now and then, looking at shadows and things that were moving. Would a ghost visit the performance? Would it become part of the performance? I'm sure most of the people in the audience were at the show for just one performance. I was hoping for two.

Ellen the ghost, as she is called at the Opera House, might have been watching in the wings, or floating across the balcony (closed to audience members). I was tempted to bring my camera in, hoping to take a picture or two of the specter. But somehow I didn't think the actors on stage would appreciate that, having this guy wandering around taking snapshots of dark corners in the room. Come to think of it, I don't think the audience members would like it either, blinding them with my flash as I try to capture an apparition floating above their heads.

Like a good boy, I kept my flash at bay, waiting until the end of the show to check for paranormal activity. The only strange incident I noticed during the play was a weird flying object (WFO?) hovering above the audience during the first Act. The best way to explain it was that it looked like a large heavy insect, fluttering aimlessly back and forth in front of the bank of lights. The weird thing was that it had this long tail, maybe eighteen inches long.

I'm convinced it was just a fly or perhaps a moth, and the tail thing was an optical illusion. It must have been my mind playing tricks on me in the darkness. I mentioned it to someone working at the play and they remarked that others have seen strange things floating above the audience. So maybe it wasn't my imagination. Perhaps it was a miniature Rodan swooping above the audience, waiting for a tiny Godzilla to come bursting through the door.

With the play finished and the audience departed, Twin Cities Paranormal Society (TCPS) moved in. We used the Opera House where the play was as the base operations point. Being that there were half a dozen other locations to investigate, they had to pick somewhere to setup base operations. The Opera House had plenty of room to store equipment and relax in between investigative sessions.

It was probably a good thing TCPS came in after the show, with their cases of equipment and cameras; the audience members would have been freaked out and never watched the play. They'd be looking in the corners of the theater for ghastly figures and glowing orbs (like I was). Not at all conducive to the actors on stage. Of course, the actors were probably more worried about Ellen the ghost playing with the lighting system, as she has done so many times before.

TCPS cofounders Lisa and Michelle ran the investigation which included a group of about ten members. The investigations would span two nights, Friday and Saturday. There were several buildings to inspect, so the ten members split into several two- or three-member teams. This is normal protocol; you never want to be investigating by yourself. One reason is for basic validity of personal experiences. It helps if more than one individual has the same experience, or can at least relate to the same experience at the time.

The other reason for using multiple members at each location is for safety reasons, in case you get hurt tromping around in an attic or basement with the lights off. The last thing you need is to have fallen, breaking your leg and have nobody there to help. You'd end up with a few hours of moaning on your audiotape, but instead of ghosts, it would be you.

Speaking of audio tapes, that night we used lots of standard equipment, Digital Audio Recorders, Flash Cameras, Video Recorders with night vision (infrared), Electro-Magnetic Field (EMF) monitors, and Digital Thermometers. With all the equipment, it's hard to believe anything could get past us, even a ghost. But my personal favorite device to use, is myself. A physical breathing human being. To me, your own personal experiences are the best barometer for hunting ghosts. There's nothing like the hair on your neck standing up as a ghostly spirit enters the room.

Most people just shrug off those personal hair-raising experiences. Not paranormal investigators. Lisa was very clear to report any unusual feelings while searching. It's usually an indicator that something has arrived in the room, even if all the techno-gadgets are reading nil. Interestingly enough, that spine tingling feeling typically arrived on somebody just before an event.

For Friday night, two buildings were chosen to investigate; the Mantorville Opera House and the Restoration House. Both buildings have had paranormal activity, although the Opera House's events were much more recent. What was explained to me was that the more recent the activity, the more likely you will encounter an event. Made sense to me, although it made me wonder about what the ghosts do in between hauntings. Play Parcheesi perhaps?

I was assigned to Lisa's group and we started up in the dressing room area of the Opera House. The women's dressing room to be exact (I chuckled at the thought of seeing a half-dressed ghost running across the room, screaming that she was late for her next performance). The other groups split up, covering the Restoration House, the basement of the Opera House, and the main floor of the Opera House. If there were ghosts lingering on the premises, we'd find them.

The first step in conjuring up a link with the spirits of the dead involves ten minutes of silence (I never asked why it was ten minutes. Why not five? Or twenty? Is there a point where if you wait too long, the ghosts will leave?). The period of silence is really more for us living investigators than the spirits. It takes several minutes for your eyes to adjust and your heart beat to slow down. But it may also give a chance for the ghosts to relax, allowing them to come out and see us (yes, even ghosts can be afraid).

The most alarming point in the investigation is that first minute of silence, where all the lights have just been turned off. There's nothing like sitting in a haunted house with all the lights off, waiting for something to jump out at you. I found myself closing my eyes, not wanting to find anything. Sure, call me a chicken. But it was creepy there in the pitch-black darkness and silence. I suppose I've seen too many horror movies. I kept waiting for some ghastly white figure to scream at me and knock me over.

That's the weird part about paranormal investigations—you're actually there, sitting in the dark, looking for demons and ghosts, trying to capture a glimpse of one. Can you say lunatic? But it's a serious matter. There are ghosts out there, some good and some bad. You also have a group of professionals trying to help you—and the ghosts. That's reassuring to know that when strange things happen, you can pick up the phone or send an email to a group like TCPS and they'll help.

So for the first ten minutes of the investigation, we had the lights out. I cheated a bit, though. I had my video camera with night vision running, so I could see things with its infrared light. Although I'm not sure if it really helped. My eyes were glued to the viewfinder, just waiting for something to jump out of the darkness. Maybe do a dance or something across the viewing area. I could handle that. But if some ghostly demon apparition floated into the camera, headed for me, I'd just plain freak out. I'd wonder where the heck it came from, but more importantly where it was going. The last thing I wanted was some beastly spirit thing passing through my body and sending chills deep into my bones. But I knew that was always a possibility.

Nothing terribly spooky happened at first. Once the ten minutes of silence was over, we started asking some questions to the spirits. *What's your name? How old are you? Did you live here? Can we help you?* We also impressed upon the spirits that we were not there to harm them. Some investigators like to come across harsh and aggravating, attempting to provoke the spirit out of hiding. I'm not sure about you, but I could do without getting the spirits all angry and having them scare the heck out of me. So, thank you very much TCPS for being nice and polite to the ghosts.

As we started asking questions, right away the hair on the back of my neck stood up. Normally I'd blow off the sensation, but being that I was in a known haunted building and in total darkness, I perked up. Interestingly enough, another member mentioned she had the exact same feeling. We started taking pictures, hoping to capture some snapshots of the paranormal event. But the feeling quickly went away after we took a few pictures. The thought was that the pictures spooked the ghost (yes, like I said, ghosts get spooked, too).

On a previous investigation at the Opera House for TCPS, many cameras would malfunction, not being able to take pictures. Strangely enough, when they 'asked' the spirits if they could take pictures, the cameras started working again. Interesting that I have a hard enough time working with cameras, just trying to find the button to focus and click in the dark. All I need is for a ghost to be getting in my way, further hindering me with my camera. Maybe the next time I'm taking pictures on a family vacation and the camera won't work, I'll blame it on the ghosts. Maybe I'll then try 'asking' for permission to use the camera.

Other than that spooky feeling, nothing else occurred up in the dressing room. I was feeling somewhat cocky with my night vision ghost-busting video camera, so I decided to walk down the hallway in the dark. I can't say that I found any ghoulish apparitions, but I did learn how difficult it was to walk in the dark while holding a camera. Several times I found myself banging my shins on things along the wall, and wondering where I was. At one point I got freaked out by a painting of a man on the wall. I thought it was a doorway. I brought my camera around stared directly into a face I wasn't expecting. Let's just say I nearly had to change my pants on that event.

A little gun-shy from my painting-of-a-man incident, I cautiously shuffled farther down the hallway to the middle room where all the costumes were stored. I took one step into the room and immediately felt spooked. Chills and all. I quickly backed out of the room. I learned that there's certain times during an investigation where you just don't feel right, and you have to make a choice. You either continue on, or back off. I backed off. At least from the room. That inner voice was saying, "Nope. I don't think you want to go in there right now." Of course, it could have been a polite suggestion from a spirit in the room, wanting some privacy. I'm sure it was not enjoying all the activity late at night, with all the paranormal investigators walking around.

After about forty-five minutes, the teams switched and I found myself in jail. No, really. It was a jail—in the basement of the Restoration House. Apparently, it had been used as a temporary jail back in the late 1800s. I went from a spooky dressing room to a spooky basement jail. I was feeling kind of cocky again (never a good way to deal with ghosts), so I chose to hang out inside the jail cell. I think if I were someone who has seen many ghosts and experienced a ton of investigations, I wouldn't have been so cocky. Visions of terror did cross my mind from time to time, as I thought about old horror movies where the guy sits in the jail cell and the big iron door slams shut and he's stuck inside with some demonic spirit. I was hoping that would not be the case for me.

Fortunately, that never happened to me in the jail cell. The worst part was sitting on the edge of the iron bed, wondering if at any moment something in the dark was going to tickle my legs or pull on my dangling feet. Worse yet, I was concerned something might jump out of the toilet at me like in the movie *Ghoulies*. Nothing like that happened. Other than a few possible shadows we thought we saw in the corner of the basement, and some interesting temperature fluctuations, our stay was uneventful. At one point one of the investigators had the feeling there was someone staring at her from outside the jail. She was sitting inside looking out. We took some pictures, and later checked audio/video, but nothing showed up.

Upstairs in the Restoration House was similar. The most terrifying part of the house was with all the mannequins and dolls. Every room had some plastic mannequin dressed up and looking right at you. I had thoughts of Chucky the demonic doll racing through my head as we walked from room to room. We did not find any obvious paranormal activity, but did have several personal experiences. Later on when reviewing the videotape, I could swear the arms on the mannequins would move slightly. And every once in a while the eyes would move. I conclude that it's just an illusion, the way things look while trying to film in darkness with infrared night vision. Still, perhaps they were moving? Perhaps they were annoyed that we were there, knowing that late at night was their time to move about the place.

It was nearing the end of the night, past 2 A.M., and our team ended up back at the Opera House. We checked out the theater area and balcony, sitting there in total darkness for a good forty minutes. There had been sightings of Ellen the ghost sitting in the front few rows of the theater, stage right. I setup my camera to look directly at the location, hoping to catch a glimpse of her. I did not find anything later on while reviewing the tape, but I did find out how creaky the floors were.

I was stationed up in the balcony during the investigation with my audio recorder and camera. I knew my video recorder down on the stage was running low, with only about fifteen minutes left. After fifteen minutes, I walked down the steps and to the front of the theater. It was a long walk, knowing that I was probably freaking out the team in the basement. The creaking was so loud, I probably bothered the team back in the Restoration House down the street. But those things happen during an investigation, and it's important to take note of that when reviewing tapes later. TCPS took many notes, detailing exactly what was happening and when. That helps later when reviewing video and audio for any mysterious activities. Otherwise, you'll think you came up with this incredible evidence of a ghost walking across the floor, but it turns out to be a real person.

Sitting up in the balcony where the spooky lighting activity occurs made me nervous. Especially when nobody else volunteered to be up there. I later found out another team saw ghostly shadows lurking up in the balcony area. If I would have known that, I would have picked a more peaceful place to investigate. Still, we were all there to find out about ghosts. That was our job (well, my job was actually to write about them, not actually find them). As I sat up in the balcony, I watched the lighting board, waiting for the sliders to move. They never did. The only weird thing that happened while I was up there was with the feeling someone was coming up the stairs. I had my back to the stairs (yeah, I know—bad idea), and at one point, it seemed like I could feel air moving up from the stairs, and perhaps even the creaking of the steps. But every time I turned around to look, nothing was there. Although while reviewing videotapes later, I heard something that sounded like a woman's voice. Couldn't quite make out what she was saying, but the voice sounded very near. There was nobody else up there except me. The nearest person was over a hundred feet away.

Back room in basement of Mantorville Opera House, right before the eerie feeling of a ghostly presence hit.

The basement in the Opera House was the creepiest place. I don't think I want to go back down there. It definitely gave me an eerie feeling. But I was still feeling a little cocky, so I decided to cover the back room, where lots of previous paranormal activity had occurred. I had my video camera zipping away, filming anything that would come in or out of the room. I also put my audio recorder in there, which was an eerie experience in itself. Walking into the pitch-black room was fine—it's when you turn and walk out. That's the scary part. You feel like there's someone right behind you. I found myself backing out of rooms many times that night. (Of course, who's to say the ghost wasn't behind me when I backed out).

I heard about cameras malfunctioning, or batteries draining when on paranormal investigations. I figured it was always some lame photographer who couldn't work the camera, or put old batteries in. Well, I at least know how to push a button on the camera, but that wouldn't even work down in the back room of the basement. I stood there in the doorway, taking two pictures with flash. No problem. Then I had this heavy feeling, as if the air in the room was getting thick. Then my camera stopped working. I looked at it several times, but each time I pressed the button, no flash—and no picture. Of course, once I got out of the basement, the camera started working again.

The scariest part of the night for me was in the back room of the basement at the Opera House. I was standing there, video taping the room, when all of a sudden I felt this ominous presence inches from my face. The hair on my neck jumped straight up. I froze, unable to move due to fear. It's hard to explain, but it felt like some guy, about six-foot-five, was bent over staring at my face (or perhaps he was shorter but floating in the air near me). Actually, it seemed like he wore a mask, one of those plastic masquerade masks, semi-translucent, held up near my face. It really didn't feel threatening, but it definitely gave me the creeps.

I could feel the presence of something near me, and my initial reaction was to turn and peer into the darkness next to me. But I didn't want to. I just kept staring into my video recorder and backed out of the room. I was done with my investigating; thankfully TCPS was done for the night too. They would continue their investigating Saturday night. On a previous visit, one of the investigators had the chair they were sitting on move across the room. Hopefully, more fascinating things like that would show up on Saturday for them. Although I'm not sure if I want to be the one sitting in the chair.

At the time of this writing, I did not get a full recap from TCPS of their Saturday night investigation. But I was told it was interesting to say the least, with several paranormal events occurring. They were investigating several other buildings around Mantorville, including the Historical Society. Apparently there is a grave on the site, possibly underneath the front porch. There is also an old lead box, casket sized, on the property as well. Many people have reported strange things happening in the building.

All in all, it was a fascinating investigation. No, we didn't capture any apparitions on film, but we did find lots of personal activity and a few interesting EVPs. To give you an example of what the night went like for me, I've included some of my notes from the evening, detailing some of the possible EVPs that I think occurred.

Tape 14, Opera House Upstairs Women's Dressing Room

04:35: Woman's voice, *'Don't be in there'*.

13:36: Soft whispering voice. Words are undecipherable.

18:01: TCPS asks for spirit to make a sound. Whispering word is heard, *'Enough'*.

19:06: TCPS asks for spirit's name. Whispering word is heard, but undecipherable.

19:36: TCPS says spirit can dance on stage with actors. A faint word is heard, *'Yes'*.

25:24: TCPS says to shut camera off. Whispering word is heard, *'No'*.

Tape 15, Opera House Upstairs Women's Dressing Room.

04:10: TCPS asks if spirit is back. A quick, high voice/moan is heard.

06:10: TCPS tells spirit we are here to help. Echoing voice is heard, *'Thank you'*.

09:33: Unknown voice saying, *'You have not'*.

As you can see, there was a lot of EVP activity up in the dressing room. I find it very interesting that no matter where you go, and what time of day it is, you can capture some interesting sounds on you digital audio recorder. I suggest you try it for yourself. Record an empty room during the day. Or perhaps record your bedroom while you sleep (ignoring the snoring though). If you have a digital recorder with a USB cable, you can quickly plug it into your computer and download it.

I use Audacity, a free editor and recorder to watch the audio recordings. I say 'watch' because it translates the audio signal into graphic images on your computer. That way you can see tiny blips of sound you may not normally catch with your ears. Give it a try. You may be surprised at what you hear.

Chapter 12

Orphan Tunnels

"...as we got closer, the hairs on our neck began to rise. I knew it was ghost time again."

Location: Owatonna

I'll admit, being an orphan at an orphanage is not the best life. But it has its benefits. That is if you like being terrified by ghosts in dark tunnels.

I was sent to the orphanage in Owatonna when I was eight years old. The word orphanage wasn't used; the correct title was, State Public School for Dependent and Neglected Children. That pretty much summed it up. Dependent and neglected.

It wasn't my fault. My parents couldn't afford to keep me. At least that's what I've come to believe. One minute I was with my parents, helping keep our farm running in western Minnesota, just outside of Worthington. The next minute it was all gone.

My dad took off, leaving Mom to take care of my sister, Claire, and me by herself. Within weeks, I could tell Mom wasn't going to make it. It was the 1920s. The stock market crashed, and the small plot of land we farmed dried up. Claire and I found ourselves shipped off to Owatonna.

There was some comfort in having Claire along with me. At least a little piece of family was coming along. "What's gonna happen, Henry?" she would say to me every five minutes on the train ride to the orphanage.

"It'll be fine, Claire. Just keep a stiff upper lip and things will go our way." I was lying of course. I had no idea what would happen to us. For all I knew we were being sent to some child labor camp where we would work the rest of

West Hills, Owatonna. Was once an orphanage for thousands of boys and girls, with several hundred never leaving, buried in a cemetery on site.

our lives away. I would have gladly done that in exchange for keeping Claire. Sadly, she was gone within a few days, adopted by a family. I was left alone now, with no family of my own. I would surely end up like one of those poor boys buried in the children's cemetery on campus, unclaimed and unwanted by any family.

After a few weeks, I learned to deal with the orphanage and the lack of a family. The boys at the orphanage became my new family. We found lots of exciting things to do. Especially with the tunnels. They were the coolest thing I'd ever seen, letting you travel from one building to another in the middle of winter, all warm and cozy. That was until we met a ghost down there.

I was running late to dinner and decided to take a short cut through the tunnels. There was one passage we were not allowed to go through, for fear it might cave in. I took my chances and squeezed through the closed gate. What surprised me most was how cold the tunnel was. All the other ones were quite warm. What I didn't understand was that the chilling air was from the apparition I just about ran over while running around a corner. It looked like a boy, a little older than myself, dressed in late 1800s knickers and a tucked-in nightshirt. He just looked at me, staring with deeply saddened eyes, as if all hope had been drained from his body.

They say the hair on the back of you neck stands straight up when a ghost is nearby. That part is true. What they never talk about is that you can easily wet your pants. I did. Let's just say I was the talk of the orphanage days to follow when I came running into the dining hall screaming with wet pants. After changing my clothes, I discussed the ghost with one of my friends, Jimmy.

"You saw a real ghost?" said Jimmy, amazed at my statement.

"Yep," I replied, very proud of my accomplishment, even if it did cost me an embarrassing moment. I proceeded to describe the ordeal to Jimmy, leaving no details out. I embellished a few parts too, just to make the story a bit more fantastical. Jimmy's eyes were as wide as baseballs.

"Let's go back there!" he said, eager to see the apparition. I, on the other hand, had no desire to soil my shorts again. But I was willing to watch Jimmy do it. "Sure, let's check it out. We'll go tonight."

That night I met Jimmy down in the basement of the main building, just past the butcher shop and bakery. Of course, Jimmy wasn't the only one there. He had in turn told half the orphanage it seemed like. I counted six of us.

"Come on," I said to them, trying to act tough. "We have to get down and back before curfew at ten P.M."

We didn't get far before we started having that weird feeling, as if somebody or something was watching us.

"Do any of you guys have goose bumps on your arms?" asked one of the boys. All of them nodded, including me. I knew what was next. Except there was no full-bodied apparition this time. All we could hear were other children laughing. They seemed to be right in front of us. We stepped closer, but every time the laughter would drift further down the tunnel.

After a few minutes of following the ghostly laughter, it disappeared. That's when we realized we were lost. To make matters worse, the lights went off.

There were several shrieks in the darkness, but none of them were from ghosts. It was several of the boys, screaming at the lack of light.

"What's gonna happen, Henry?" said one of them. I felt like they were my sister, Claire, afraid and asking for help.

"I don't know," I said. It was the truth. But I had an idea.

As our eyes adjusted to the darkness, we began to see a faint glimmer of light in one direction. We agreed that it was a light source probably from an open door or ventilation shaft. We slowly shuffled our way toward the light, but as we got closer, the hairs on our neck began to rise. I knew it was ghost time again.

We reached the light source and found it to be a ventilation shaft reaching up to the bright moonlit night. The fresh air and light were immediately gratifying, giving us some hope that we would be all right. That didn't last long, as a tingling feeling deepened, going through our toes as we looked to the right down another tunnel.

It was a ghostly funeral procession of small caskets; each floating by themselves and each opened to reveal a child in them. We watched, too horrified to move as dozens floated by us, down the end of the tunnel and vanishing into the wall.

"It's the cemetery," Jimmy said, breaking the deathly silence. Everyone turned to him as the last casket went by. "The Children's Cemetery. It's in that direction. They're going there to be buried."

That was too much for me. Thinking about the several hundred children that had died at the orphanage was terrifying, especially knowing most died with no family to turn to. It was more horrifying than the ghosts.

Wondering if more ghosts were to appear, and still not quite sure which way to go in the darkness, we huddled underneath the ventilation shaft. Just when all hope was lost, the lights finally turned back on. One of the boys immediately recognized where we were, seeing a sign on the wall, and it didn't take any discussion as what to do next. We ran. Nobody wanted to spend one more second down in the tunnels, especially if the lights went off again.

We made it back just before curfew. Unfortunately, a janitor caught us sneaking back in. That gave us three weeks of kitchen duty and bathroom cleaning. None of us were that upset with the punishment. As long as we didn't have to go back into those tunnels. From that day forward we never stepped foot in the tunnels at night. Rarely during the day for that matter—even in January. We figured our chances were much better with the frostbite of a cold Minnesota winter than with the ghostly coffins floating through the tunnel.

I'm all grown up now and have lived a long life. I've heard stories about the Owatonna orphanage being haunted. Mysterious laughter from children that are no longer there, books and things moving around on their own. I know for a fact it's all true. I've seen it with my own eyes. From time to time I visit the place, being that it's really the only spot I can call home. I even stop by the Children's Cemetery to pay my respects. I know a few of the children buried there. I wonder if they're still haunting the tunnels and buildings, looking for their family, or anyone they can call family.

History:

The orphanage started in 1886, its official title was the State Public School for the Dependent and Neglected Children. Regardless of the name, it was an orphanage. Children arrived from across the Midwest, all unfortunate enough to have lost their parents. Over ten thousand children have come and gone through the walls of its campus before it closed down in 1945, but some say a few children never left.

The orphanage was virtually self-sufficient, with buildings that housed sleeping quarters, kitchens, a power plant, icehouse, fruit cellar, bakery, barber, and butcher shop. They even had acreage to farm, bringing in lots of fruits, grains, and vegetables. For the less fortunate, a cemetery was created in the southwest corner of the campus area.

Over 300 children died while staying at the orphanage, most being buried in the cemetery and with no family to claim them. Funerals were held on stage in one of the buildings for all the children to see. Perhaps that's the main reason for the haunting, with so many children who died, unclaimed by their families, they sadly roam the campus, forever searching for a family of their own.

There were also many tunnels that connected the buildings together. In the harsh Minnesota winters, being able to travel in warmth from one building to the next was essential. Most of the tunnels were used by the employees to get from their living quarters to where they worked on site.

Since the orphanage closed in 1945, the buildings have been used as office space, a museum, and apartments. During this time, many people have experienced strange activity that they cannot explain.

Reports claim that ghosts of orphaned children haunt the more than dozen buildings that used to be the orphanage. In particular, the third floor of the main building has had several incidents.

Witnesses have seen the wooden floorboards warp right in front of their eyes, as if they were melting. Others have complained of a heavy cigar smoke filtering through the air, even though nobody has smoked cigars in the building for years. Severe temperature changes have occurred, where the temperature has plummeted by more than twenty degrees.

The tunnels are especially eerie. Employees currently working in the buildings will occasionally hear the sound of children laughing from down in the tunnels. Sometimes you can hear them from the ventilation shafts above ground. Strange lights have also been known to come from the tunnels, even when nobody is in there.

The Owatonna Police have had phone calls from the main building at night, as if somebody were calling for help. The police would rush out to the building, only to find it quiet and dark. This has happened several times.

A janitor working late at night has had books moved around from shelf to shelf while he's working there. He's claimed that other things like chairs have been known to move around on their own. Doors will mysteriously open and close by themselves. He's also seen lights come back on late at night, after turning them off early in the evening.

Even the apartments across the street have had strange occurrences. Someone reported that his brother-in-law who was sleeping in an apartment bedroom face down began to feel like a small child was walking or dancing on his back. It felt like tiny feet running up and down the length of his body, and across the bed as well. He quickly turned around to see what it was, but nothing was there.

A girl in another apartment of the same building was sitting on the floor watching TV. She noticed a reflection in a nearby mirror of someone walking behind her down the hallway. When she turned around, nobody was there. At first she thought it was her mom (who was the only other person in the apartment at the time). But she discovered that her mom was in her bedroom resting, not having walked through the apartment for some time.

Lights in the apartments will go on and off all by themselves. Sometimes tenants will leave for work in the morning checking to make sure all the lights are off. When they come home at the end of the day, some lights are back on. This has happened several times. Occasionally, the lights

An apartment in West Hills that is reported to be haunted with children from the old orphanage.

will come back on only after a few minutes of being off. A few times, the lights will turn on while they're in the room, sleeping at night.

Field Trip:

When you first drive up to the place, you get an impressive feeling, like you're coming up to some amazing estate.

Then you remember that thousands of children lived there, with nowhere else to go. That made me feel sad and depressed. It hit me pretty hard as I stood outside the main building and read the plaques that described what it was like back when it was first an orphanage. It didn't sound like the greatest place to live, but for the boys and girls living there, they had no other choice.

My first stop was checking out the inside. I would have loved to go up to the third floor where so much activity had occurred. Sadly, I did not have that opportunity. After a moment or two inside the main building, I left to wander around among the other buildings. Keep in mind, the orphanage, at one point, had forty-two acres of building sites, so there was plenty to look at.

With my digital recorder in hand, and camera in the

One of the vent shafts connected to the underground tunnels.

other, I walked around, checking out the various buildings. Most of my tour, I felt nothing unusual or eerie. But I had the impression this would be an incredible site to check out at night with experienced paranormal investigators. With the numerous buildings and the interconnecting tunnels, there was bound to be some ghostly activity somewhere. When I came to a vent shaft for the tunnels, I knew something was here.

I had that feeling as I peered down through bars into the shaft that something was down there. It was definitely a place to investigate. As I stared down into the tunnel, I wondered how many children had run through them, laughing and giggling as they played in the dimly lit area. I'm sure they had to find ways to enjoy themselves, and running around in the tunnels was probably a highlight.

The other creepy part of my walk was over in the southwest corner of the campus area. That's where the cemetery is. I couldn't really see it at first, but I felt like something interesting was there. The fruit cellar was there that gave me an eerie feeling as well. I could imagine sitting out in the cemetery at night, waiting for the ghostly children to appear. Spooky indeed.

I went across the street to see the apartments with the paranormal activity. I took a couple pictures and one of them had a strange orange glow coming from a window. It had to be a reflection of some sort, or was it? I looked around for something orange in the trees or driveway, but there wasn't anything.

I'd have to say that the old orphanage certainly has the potential to be haunted, but the only way in my opinion to verify that is to have a paranormal investigation. I wouldn't mind helping out, but I don't think I want to be the guy stuck down in the tunnels.

Chapter 13
Parks of Panic

"The orange lights were spooky, and walking through the forest at night was definitely not a walk in the park."

Cashman Park in Owatonna, one of several reported parks that are haunted by restless spirits.

Location: Owatonna

Some say drinking alcohol is bad for you. I happen to know for a fact that it can be even worse if you're out at a secluded park partying among angry ghosts.

My friend, Brian, had a party planned for us senior high school students at a nearby park in Owatonna Friday night.

"Everyone will be there, Tom," he said. He always said that. But this time was different. This time Hannah was supposed to show up, the hottest girl at Owatonna High School.

"Sounds great," I said. "What will you have to drink?"

He smiled and said, "Good stuff." That meant his older brother was involved, no doubt bringing beer. Brian's brother was twenty-one, old enough to get us a few cases of beer.

"Where's the party at?"

"Cashman." Cashman Park, one of the creepiest places to stay out late and party at. Brian always had that kind of class.

Friday night couldn't have arrived any sooner. It was a tough week, with mid-semester tests hitting everybody hard. It was our last year in high school and we wanted to relax and hangout together, drinking a few beers and enjoying the night. Of course, someone should have told the ghosts. Or perhaps someone should have warned us not to party at Cashman Park late at night.

I pulled up in my Jeep just as the sun was setting. Walking up the path from the Cashman Park sign always gave me the creeps, even during the day. It was as if you were walking into another world, transcending from civilization to an ancient world filled with nothing but the wind and trees. I often wondered what it was like living back a hundred years, or two hundred even. Strolling through Cashman Park gave me a hint of what it must have been like.

As I took the winding path up through the woods, I began to see the faint flickering light of a fire. I could hear Brian's voice, and his older brother David. A few others had shown up already and were sampling David's beer selection.

"Ahhh!" said Brian after he chugged one of the beers. He then belched out, "Miller Lite!" Several others joined in with belching, "Good beer... Nice flavor... Party..." Eventually, everyone was trying to belch out the alphabet. Lots of male testosterone was flying, with belching, head butting, and loud obnoxious bragging about girls. That's of course when Hannah and her friends arrived.

Everyone went silent, surprised that the girls even showed up. Brian was not the most popular guy in school by far. But he did have an older brother who was. And brought beer.

It didn't take long for the girls to corner David, asking him about college and other things. David loved every minute of it, until he remembered these were seventeen year olds. The last thing David wanted was to end up in jail, never finishing his college career.

"We'll see you girls later," said David as he pushed his way through the floating mob of teenage girls. He smiled at them and added, "When you're eighteen." He then turned to Brian and I in front of the campfire and said, "You guys have fun out here with all the spooks."

"Yeah, right," said Brian as he finished another beer, crumpling the can and throwing it in the fire. A big billowing flame erupted from the fire as the can knocked a loose log over. It made everyone jump back, as if some ghostly apparition had just flown by and commanded the flames to rise.

"You see! The Indians are restless here!" said David as he raised his hands over the fire, mocking the tall flame that flickered into the air.

Brian just shook his head at his brother's lame attempt to be scary. He said to David while pointing to the underage girls, "Maybe you need to stay and protect us, or at least your girl groupies over there."

David turned to Hannah and the girls, who were still gawking over him from a distance. "Yeah, well, I think I better be going." He started to walk away, then turned back to us and said, "Just don't get any of the ghosts mad. You know, this is the site of an Indian massacre back a hundred and fifty years ago." David paused to absorb everyone's expressions. They instantly became silent with every head turned toward him. They were obviously interested in his story. "In fact, I think it was in October, this very night possibly. Yeah, I'd watch out if I were you. Keep an eye out for those flying tomahawks." David walked away from the campfire, chuckling at their wide eyes and open mouths.

I hadn't thought much about it, but standing out in the woods, knowing there were dead bodies littering the area years ago gave me the creeps. Just then were heard a blood curdling scream from the darkness. "Eeeaahhhhh!!!" Everyone shuffled in closer to the fire. Then someone leaped from the darkness, landing right in front of us. I nearly had a heart attack.

"Aha! Gotcha!" it yelled. Everyone breathed a sigh of relief, realizing it was just David. He was obviously amused with our sudden fear of the night as he laughed hysterically for a moment at us before finally leaving, this time for good.

The best thing about David's scare was that it brought the girls closer to us. I have to give him credit for that part. But he spooked all of us, and for some reason we didn't feel like hanging out and just drinking beer anymore. Instead, we started telling ghost stories. Yeah, I know. We were spooked enough already. But like I said, it was bringing the girls in closer, and Hannah was sitting right next to me.

The stories raised hairs on the back of our necks and arms numerous times. Stories started with vampires and werewolves, but turned quickly to more realistic tales of zombies and haunted houses. It wasn't until we started talking about ghostly cemeteries and spooky parks did we get really scared. Especially when we starting hearing things in the darkness.

"Did you hear something?" I asked to Hannah. I wasn't sure if I heard anything, but I was certainly trying to strike up a conversation with her.

"I think so," she said while moving closer to me. Restless spirits or not, this night was turning into one of the best of my life. That is until we heard the moaning.

After a brief pause, Brian yelled into the shadows, "Okay, David. We've had enough of your jokes." Everyone waited for a response, some kind of 'Gotcha!' to come from the blackness. But it never came.

There were several moans now, all of them getting louder, as if something was coming toward us. Thoughts of *Night of the Living Dead* movie we recently rented came to mind. Could there be zombies coming at us?

"I don't like this," said Hannah, who now hugged my arm. *I like this,* I thought. *I very much like having Hannah hugging me.* I didn't like the moaning sounds though. They sounded like somebody was in a lot of pain.

"Look over there!" said Brian, pointing far into the dark forest. A faint, orange glow could be seen far off the trail. The spot got bigger, as if someone were coming closer.

"What do we do?" asked Hannah.

Brian replied, "I think we should split up. In case it's a policeman with a flashlight."

"You mean police*men,*" I said. "Now there's more than one light." You could now see several of these little orange glowing lights. There must have been at least a dozen.

"That's a lot of police. I think we better make a run for it," said Brian.

I quickly added, "Are you nuts? It's pitch black out here and none of us brought any flashlights."

"Well, do you have a better idea?" asked Brian.

I did, but what I really wanted to do was stay here with Hannah. I looked up at the glowing lights. They were getting closer. Twenty meters away perhaps. "I think we should calmly head down the path out of the park."

"What, and run right into the police waiting at the end? No way." Brian got up to leave, flipping on a light. "I brought a flashlight, and I'm heading out that way." He pointed into the woods, the opposite from where the glowing orange lights were coming from. Most everyone stood up and began following Brian into the woods. I reluctantly followed. Unfortunately, we didn't get far.

I looked behind us, worried the orange lights would quickly follow us, but they were gone. "Say, Brian. Where did the lights go? Brian?" Everyone stopped moving and looked forward. I turned to look ahead and realized where the orange glowing lights went. They were in front of us now.

"So much for sneaking away," I said.

"Now what do we do!" asked Hannah, who was still by my side, holding my hand.

"I think we should head back and walk out on the trail," said Brian. Yeah, what a brilliant plan. Exactly what I had said in the first place. But I wasn't going to complain. The orange lights were spooky, and walking through this forest at night was definitely not a walk in the park.

I had flashes of *Blair Witch Project* movie, wondering when the wicked witch would come out. Then the lights began to move fast. Real fast. They were rotating around us in a counter-clockwise motion, faster and faster until it was almost as if a solid ring of orange light surrounded us. The shining lights were only a few meters out, but then they began to shrink, moving in to within only a few feet of us. I looked into the spinning orange glow and thought I could see silhouettes of people. Were they from the Native American massacre of one hundred and fifty years ago? Were they coming back for revenge? I didn't want to stick around and find out.

"I don't like the looks of this!" yelled Brian, who picked up a rock and threw it at the light. Big mistake. I think that was the point at which we made the ghosts mad.

The spinning light stopped, leaving us with the glow of Brian's flashlight and the campfire. That is until his batteries went dead. Then the fire mysteriously went out. That's when the panic hit.

Have you ever wanted to run through a forest at breakneck speed, blindfolded? I don't recommend trying it. But that's what it was like for us. Afterwards I'll admit it must have sounded funny. Boys screaming like girls, and girls screaming like, well, girls. All of us running around bumping into each other, trees, and of course, ghosts.

Yes, ghosts. Something was out there besides us, and they weren't happy. We never saw them, but we heard them. Loud, ear splitting Native American war cries, sounding out from every direction. I imagined this was how General Custer felt at his Last Stand. There was no way to run without bumping into someone or something, and hearing war cries, horse galloping, and I think I even heard tomahawks whizzing by our heads. I wasn't sure, but I knew I wasn't going to stick around to find out.

Thankfully, the incident only lasted about a minute. But that was enough for me. The yelling and screaming stopped, the fire came back, and Brian's flashlight started working again.

Throughout the whole ordeal, Hannah was still holding onto my hand, clawing me in a rigid death-grip that left deep gouges in my hand for days. That was fine with me. It gave me something to talk about with her later on. Although nobody wanted to discuss what happened that night for weeks. In fact, to this day it's hard to talk about, let alone visit Cashman Park again. At least not at night. You never know if the restless ghosts will come to life and visit with you—war cries and all.

History:

It's interesting to note that there are many ghost stories coming from parks in Owatonna. More so than from any other location I researched in Southeastern Minnesota. Especially when you compare it to other 'normal' ghost stories, from buildings and cemeteries. The majority of the paranormal activity described came from public parks. Three notable parks in particular are Mineral Springs Park, Cashman Park, and Kaplan Woods Park.

Mineral Springs Park

Mineral Springs Park, located on the east end of town, was apparently the home of some Native Americans back in the 1880s. They enjoyed the spot due to the mineral springs located there. The water from the springs was supposed to be refreshing and bring youthful energy to the Native Americans. Perhaps there was a battle there between tribes, fighting for the rights to use the springs.

Eventually the City of Owatonna purchased the land, turning it into a public park. Paths lead around the river that runs through it, and tall trees sprout along the banks and hillside of the park. Coming to the park during the day provides you with the opportunity to take a relaxing walk, or sit and read a favorite book underneath the pavilion. Going there at night is another story.

Sources indicate that going to Mineral Springs Park at night is not recommended. People visiting the park late at night have experienced the feeling of strong negativity, as if some ghostly presence did not want them there. Dizziness and a deep heavy pressure is said to occur. Still others have reported strange orange glows of light in the wooded area that surrounds the park. Perhaps they are the phantom torches from Native Americans traveling through the woods, or maybe they are the souls of the Native Americans themselves.

Cashman Park

Cashman Park is another haunted area, and for good reason. Apparently there was a Native American massacre at

Mineral Springs Park. Local residents say it's haunted and not to go there late at night.

the location of the park back in the late 1800s. The park is full of trails through the woods, and is a great place for a walk during the daytime. But not at night.

Nobody is safe in Cashman Park late at night. That's when it's said the spirits come out, making you feel unwelcome. Many people have had unexplainable feelings of dread and sorrow while visiting the park late at night. For that reason it is not recommended you travel through the woods in the dark hours of evening. Not only to stay away from terrifying ghosts, but also teenagers with bad intentions and possibly doing drugs.

Kaplan Woods Park

One other park is Kaplan Woods Park. People walking and jogging through the woods have had similar experiences as the other parks in Owatonna, supposedly from restless Native American spirits. Perhaps hundreds of years ago, the entire city of Owatonna once was a thriving community of Native Americans, peacefully living among the trees and rivers flowing through. Now Kaplan Woods is one of the only few places left in the area that contain some of the original forest. Perhaps the Native Americans spirits are there, making sure what little bit of land left stays like it was, pure and natural.

Other thoughts about what haunts Kaplan Woods stem from the possibility of Kaplan ancestors. They still roam the forest, enjoying a relaxing walk in the woods. They love the land and do not want to leave. Still others believe the ghosts are that of loggers who used to work there back in the 1800s. Some in the area may have died after tragic logging accidents while moving lumber down the rivers or possibly onto trains.

Regardless of what is haunting the woods, many say it is not friendly, and going there at night is not advisable.

Field Trip:

I have to say it was an interesting experience, walking through the three parks: Mineral Springs Park, Cashman Park, and Kaplan Woods Park. The best part was that I got my exercise in for the day. The worst part was that I really didn't come up with any specific paranormal activity. Still, even without any hard evidence, there were several times I did have some personal experiences. Ones that made me feel as if there may be some truth to the haunted parks.

I started in Cashman Park. It was a cloudy day, overcast at best, and a bit windy. That didn't help my attempt to capture any EVPs from wandering spirits in the park. Luckily, Cashman Park is in a forest setting, so the wind wasn't too bad. I walked for some time, taking pictures and trying to feel if there was anything weird there. I felt like the only thing odd was myself, walking through the woods by myself with a camera and recorder. I chuckled thinking about how weird it probably looked. Still, I was here to capture meaningful information about any paranormal activity.

The only point in my walk that was interesting was on the way out. Along the way, I asked if there were any restless spirits that wanted to communicate with me. Just as I asked, a loud crack sounded to my left. It was about thirty meters off the trail and it certainly spooked me. It was loud enough that it had to be something big that moved.

I figured it had to be a tree branch snapping, or a trunk cracking. With the winds blowing by, it was no doubt that. The odd thing was that in the forest area, there was not much of a wind. I'm not entirely sure what it was, and it didn't happen any other time during my walk.

I have to admit, it was very alarming to know that dozens of people died in the area from the massacre. I tried to picture the gruesome sight, dead bodies lying about. It definitely gave me the creeps. I could see why the place would be haunted, or why people think it might be.

The next park on my list was Mineral Springs Park. I walked around the area for a while, in between all of the tall hundred-year-old trees, but I came up with nothing. It was a beautiful park, with a little creek flowing through it. But nothing spooky jumped out at me. There were no EVPs on my recorder either. It definitely didn't feel spooky at all. Although that could change if I were there at night.

My final stop was at Kaplan Woods. This place definitely felt spooky at times. I could feel it as I walked into the place down the main path. The size of the park was impressive; there were several miles of walking paths, and acres of trees. Old trees that are very tall. You really felt like you were thrown back a hundred years ago, taken away from civilization.

Like I said, I got my exercise in for the day, that's for sure; I must have walked four miles just in Kaplan Woods. It really is a beautiful park. I highly recommend taking a walk through it during the day. At night, well, that's another story. I think I'd start having flashbacks from the *Blare Witch* movie. Several times during my walk in the daytime I had a strange sensation, wondering if at any point I'd suddenly find myself lost, unable to leave the park.

Kaplan Woods, a large wooded park with lots of trails, and supposedly just as many ghosts.

Chapter 14

Red Hat Boy

"...around 3 A.M. I heard the sound I didn't want to hear. Tapping at my window."

Sketch of Thorson Hall at St. Olaf College, where students report that a ghostly boy in a red hat haunts them.

Location: Northfield

I still see the eyes of the Red Hat Boy, staring down at me from Thorson Hall, as if watching and waiting for someone else to join his ranks of the undead...

St. Olaf is a fantastic college. Nestled in the hills of Northfield, up from Carlton College, its beauty and splendor pull you deep into numerous buildings filled with stories and heritage from over one hundred years back. One such story, which I now know to be true, deals with the Red Hat Boy.

When I first heard about the Red Hat Boy ghost story, my friend Sheila and I thought it was silly. It's about a ghost boy with a red baseball cap that follows you around campus late at night. But one night in our freshmen year at a September bonfire for homecoming, we saw him.

"Teresa," called my friend, Sheila. "Look, up in our window."

I looked up to our dorm room window and gasped. There was something standing, or perhaps hovering, in the window. It had what looked like a red cap on. I immediately figured she was playing a prank on me, or perhaps it was one of the girls down the hall. I pushed Sheila and said, "Nice try. You almost got me on that one."

"What do you mean? I'm serious. That Red Hat Boy is up in our window!"

She looked sincere. That's what scared me. I still didn't believe it was real, so we decided to take a break from the bonfire and head up to investigate.

Sheila's boyfriend, Jeff, came along too. That made me feel a little better. If there was something supernatural going on, it always helped to have a big hulking guy with you. As it turned out, Jeff was no help at all.

By the time we got upstairs to our dorm room and opened the door, nothing was there. I'd expected as much. Whether it was a real ghost or not, whatever it was wouldn't stay around for us to yell at it.

Of course, the Red Hat Boy wasn't entirely gone.

"Look at the window," said Sheila.

Jeff walked over, leaning forward to inspect. "Cool," he said. "There's frosted-up hand prints on the outside of the window."

"Like something was trying to get in," added Sheila.

"Great," I said, "the last thing I want to think about while trying to sleep tonight is some phantom vampire rapping at my window, like I'm in Stephen King's *Salem's Lot* novel."

Just then we heard tapping at our door. All three of us jumped and turned around. It was the Resident Advisor for the floor, Jamie.

"Try to keep it down in here. A few students living on the floor have complained about loud music in here. A Led Zeppelin song, *D'yer Mak'er* to be exact.

I looked at Sheila, then back to Jamie and said, "We don't even have that song."

Jamie just looked at us for a moment, not believing us. Then she snapped, "Either way, keep it down." She abruptly turned and walked further down the hallway.

"What crawled up her butt?" asked Jeff.

"She's always like that," replied Sheila. "You get used to it."

As Jeff was talking, I began to have an eerie feeling. The kind you get when you think somebody's watching you from behind. I instinctively turned toward the window and gasped.

"What is it?" asked Sheila, alarmed at my sudden burst of breath.

"I – I thought I saw something."

"A red hat, perhaps?" smiled Jeff.

Sheila poked him and said, "Knock it off, Jeff." She turned to me, genuinely concerned. "Are you okay, Teresa? You look like you've seen a ghost."

Several uneventful weeks passed by on campus, with no additional sightings of the Red Hat Boy. I was fine with that. I had no desire to bump into any ghosts while trying hard to get good grades. Of course, that ended up not being my choice. The Red Hat Boy appeared again to me in November, the week before Thanksgiving break.

It was in the middle of the night, around 3 A.M. I heard the sound I didn't want to hear. Tapping at my window. Sheila, sleeping comfortable due to a few sips of schnapps earlier, heard nothing.

I really didn't want to look, for fear of seeing something altogether frightening, scary enough to wet my bed. After several more taps, I got up the courage to look at the window. Thankfully, there was nothing there except a few frosty smudges on the window. *But how do you get frosty smudges on the outside of a window on a third-story building?* The prints looked like small hands, as if someone were trying to get in.

As I turned to look over at Sheila, I noticed the room to our door was open. I found that odd, knowing that I heard Sheila close and lock the door when she came in earlier. I proceeded to get out of bed and walk over to close the door, when I noticed out in the hallway someone walking around. *They were wearing a red hat.*

I gulped, terrified at the realization. There was a ghost walking down the hallway. It had to be. I should have been frozen in place, but something made me want to look. I peered into the dimly lit hallway and watched as the boy, dressed in jeans and a long trench coat jacket floated away from me. The creepiest part was that you could see right through him. He reached the end of the hallway and floated right through the wall.

That was enough for me to be convinced of ghosts. Either that or I might have still been dreaming, fitfully sleeping from the taste of too much schnapps. As I walked back to my dorm room, just about walking in, the door slammed shut. I could hear a clicking sound and immediately knew I had been locked out of my room.

To make matters worse, I didn't have my key with me. I was also in my underwear. I tapped on the door, asking Sheila to let me in. Pressing my ear to the door, I could hear Sheila inside snoring away. *Great*, I thought to myself. *Sheila's so drunk, she locked me out and is back to snoozing. And I'm stuck out here in my underwear!*

I rapped on the door harder and called for Sheila. Still no response. But I thought I could hear music coming from inside. Pachabel's *Canon in D* to be precise. It was very strange to have the music playing, especially since we didn't own that CD.

Pounding hard on the door I yelled, "Sheila!" The music stopped playing, but I couldn't hear any movement from Sheila inside. Unfortunately, practically everyone else on the floor had woken up, including Jamie.

"What's going on out here?" whispered Jamie loudly.

That's when I heard my door unlock. I smiled at Jamie and whispered back, "Nothing!" I quickly slipped through the door and locked it behind me.

The first thing I noticed was that Sheila was still sleeping in bed. *Who opened the door for me?* As if on cue, I heard tapping at the window and looked outside. It was the Red Hat Boy, hovering in front of the window.

I've screamed many times in my life, but never with such intensity. I believe I nearly shattered the window with my shriek, and any glass within a two-block radius. It also was loud enough to wake up Sheila from her schnapps slumber.

"Teresa? What is it?"

By now the Red Hat Boy was gone, only a terrifying snapshot in my memory.

"Teresa?" repeated Sheila.

I was still too petrified from fright to speak. Sheila rolled over and looked at me. I'll never forget the look on her face when she saw me. Later, she said I looked pure white, as if all the blood had drained from my face. I guess that's pretty common when seeing ghosts. I even hear your hair can turn white, and your fingernails will grow real long.

I survived the rest of the school year living in the dorms, in the same room, thankfully never seeing the Red Hat Boy again. Perhaps I scared him with my scream. Fine with me. Even now I have trouble looking out windows. This year at school I'm living off campus in a house. But to be safe, I pull the blinds down each night, making sure no Red Hat Boy will be staring in at me when I walk by.

History:

St. Olaf College has been around since 1874, originally known as an academy. By 1886, a college department was added, and soon, St. Olaf had its first college class graduates in 1890.

Most of the ghostly activities have occurred in several halls: Hilleboe, Thorson, and Melby Halls. There have also been some incidents at Kelsey Theater. The most-known story centers on confrontations that students have had with the Red Hat Boy in Thorson Hall.

Two students, living in Thorson Hall, were at a bonfire outside one night when they looked up at the window of their dorm room. They saw a small figure standing in it, wearing a red baseball cap. They shrugged it off, thinking they had looked at a different window. But more strange things began to happen.

Noises and odd occurrences began to unnerve the students. One such incident had to do with their cassette tape and CD player. Every time they tried to play Led Zeppelin's *Dy'er Mak'er*, the player would mysteriously stop. Similar incidents occurred when trying to play Pachabel's *Canon in D*. Apparently the ghost has a thing for music.

There have been apparitions seen as well. Two students woke up one night to find two ghostly young men sitting at the end of their lofts, staring at them with dark, sullen eyes. By the time the students realized what was happening, the ghosts vanished. A few nights later, one of the roommates woke up crying, obviously disturbed. At first the other roommate thought it was just a bad dream. After calming down, the sobbing roommate explained that she had seen two young men playing cards on the floor. Nobody was in the room besides the two girls, and the door was locked. The young ghostly men have shown up several times.

Other students living in Thorson Hall have even seen the Red Hat Boy's dog, a black lab, roaming around campus. The Red Hat Boy himself appears in a certain rooms. It is assumed that the rooms were where he stayed. The theory about the Red Hat Boy is that he went to college at St. Olaf years ago and stayed in Thorson Hall. He loved it there so much that even in death he wanted to continue staying there. Hilleboe Hall has had some interesting activity in the past.

A student in the dorm during the summer heard childlike singing. Piano playing was also heard, but when investigating the sounds, she found all the sinks in the rooms had been turned on. Furthermore, mysterious child-sized handprints have appeared on the outside of the third-floor windows.

In Melby Hall, the oldest hall on campus, a man and women in Victorian clothing haunt the hallways, slowly walking back and forth as if watching over everyone in the hall. Sometimes the apparitions can be found walking through doors into student rooms. Occasionally, they will be seen at the top of the stairway, looking down at you.

Kelsey Theater supposedly has the ghost of Miss Kelsey herself in it. Some students have seen Miss Kelsey playing at a piano onstage, even long after her death. Students have also heard her talking with actors who were rehearsing late at night. In one such instance Miss Kelsey yelled at an actor, warning him about falling into the orchestra pit. That warning saved the young actor from a tragic fall.

Chapter 15

Room 4450

"He got up from the desk and threw open his door. What he saw terrified him."

Richards Hall at Winona State College, one of several buildings with paranormal activity.

Location: Winona

*J*onathan wondered how he'd ended up in a cemetery. One minute he'd been sleeping soundly after studying hard for his senior year finals at Winona State College, the next minute he was walking through a cemetery. To make matters worse, it was the end of October with a chilly wind blowing by, and he was in his pajamas.

It started to come back to him. The Ouija board. The tombstone. A ghost named Ruth.

It was hard to forget Ruth. She was a ghost that regularly haunted Lourdes Hall on campus. Apparently, she used to live on the third and fourth floor, back in the 1800s.

Jonathan came wandering back into Lourdes Hall in the wee hours of the morning, still dressed in his pajamas.

"What's up with you!" said Jonathan's roommate. "And why did you head out last night like that? Your eyes looked all glazed over."

"I...I don't know," replied Jonathan. Which was true. Although he had his suspicions with Ruth and the Ouija board.

Jonathan's roommate chuckled and said, "Next time wear pants."

"Right. I'll remember that."

What worried Jonathan most was that this was not the first time he'd run off into the night. Several times he'd find himself in the hallway on the fourth floor, wandering around. Once he even made it outside, on his way to Phelps Hall before a security guard stopped him. But last night he had made it all the way to the cemetery, two miles away. That was creepy.

The next day Jonathan went to the doctor to get himself checked out. If he was turning into some sleepwalking freak, he wanted to know about it before it was too late. He worried about waking up in the middle of a busy highway, or worse yet, naked early morning in the middle of campus.

"You're a healthy young man," replied the campus doctor. "You can't be much fitter."

"Thanks, but I don't feel healthy. I keep having these sleep-walking episodes. And these really weird dreams."

"What sort of dreams? Nightmares?"

"Sort of. Spooky though. With this scary ghost lady named Ruth."

The doctor's eyes lit up, with his eyebrows rising. "Ruth did you say?"

"Yeah, Ruth. She's a ghost haunting Lourdes Hall on campus. I don't believe in ghosts, though."

"Interesting," was all the doctor would say.

Jonathan said, "Interesting in a *good* way, or a *bad* way?"

The doctor looked at Jonathan for a moment, then said, "I went to Winona State, and remember the stories about Ruth. I lived up on Lourdes Hall, fourth floor. Room 4450."

Jonathan froze when the doctor said the room number. "That's my room too."

"And supposedly that's Ruth's old room." The doctor paused a moment before adding, "the room where she jumped to her death."

The hair on the back of Jonathan's neck rose, sending a tingling sensation down through his body to his toes. *That was one of my dreams*, thought Jonathan.

"Be careful up there on the third floor," said the doctor. He remembered what he had gone through years ago while living there. He found it odd that Jonathan had come to him, of all the doctors in town, and brought up the subject of Ruth. But the doctor knew it wasn't a coincidence. He understood it was planned. Fate or destiny as one would call it. The doctor cleared his throat and added, "Be careful on the fourth floor too. Lots of strange things happen there."

"I don't believe in ghosts," said Jonathan.

The doctor led Jonathan to the door, smiled, and said, "You just may change your mind. I was the same way, until I met Ruth one night." Jonathan shook the doctor's hand and noticed a large cross dangling from a gold chain around his neck. It twinkled in the fluorescent light, flashing at Jonathan as if warning him of some impending doom. On the way home from the doctor, Jonathan bought a cross to wear. He wasn't religious at all, but he figured it couldn't hurt.

The next few days were uneventful for Jonathan; no sleepwalking or eerie dreams bothered him. About the scariest moment was getting his test scores back. He had not studied enough and was now failing his geometry class. After talking to his professor, they agreed that he could retake the test, but he would have to ace it to get a passing grade. Jonathan planned to study all night in preparation. Unfortunately for Jonathan, the ghost of Ruth had other plans.

The strange occurrences started in his room, with cold chills sprouting up making him put on a coat while he crammed for his test. The lights flickered while Jonathan reached for his calculator, only to find that it was not where he put it. He stared at his desk, searching back and forth for the missing item, then leaned to his side to look on the floor. When he looked back on the desk, the calculator was there.

Jonathan could handle misplaced items and cold chills. It could easily be written off as simple forgetfulness, or a drafty dormitory. But when he started hearing eerie voices in the hallway, all concentration on studying came to an end. He could make out a few words being said:

The baby... the baby...

At first he couldn't exactly tell what the words were. He'd walk out into the hallway to find out what was being said, but every time he went out there, the hallway was empty. The words continued:

The baby... the baby...

The voice sounded like a woman and was extremely sad. But it bothered Jonathan. He had lots of studying to do. Annoyed, he got up and checked the hallway again. Still nothing. "Go away," he mumbled to himself, thinking it was a prank from somebody down the hall. "I'm trying to study."

A few minutes later he could hear more voices outside. Jonathan couldn't tell what they were saying, but he didn't care. He had a test to study for and did not want any further interruptions. He got up from his desk and threw open his door. What he saw terrified him.

Hovering in front of his door was a nun, or at least the outline of a nun, complete with headdress and long black coat. The nun held something in her arms. It was a baby.

It must be Ruth, thought Jonathan. *And she has a baby.*

Ruth stared at Jonathan for a moment, then turned and floated away, down the hallway toward the elevator. Jonathan followed her, even with him being terrified. He couldn't help himself, as if he was mesmerized into following her.

They continued down the hallway until they reached the elevator. At that point, the elevator opened. Jonathan was expecting someone to step out, but instead the door opened to an empty shaft. Now Ruth the ghost looked deeply saddened. What happened next shocked Jonathan.

From out of the corner of his left eye he saw a black, shadowy figure racing up the hallway toward them. It moved at lightning quick speed and grabbed the phantom baby from Ruth. It then turned and leaped into the elevator shaft with the baby, floating down into the darkness. Instinctively, Jonathan jumped forward, trying to rescue the falling baby. In the process he walked right through Ruth, sending chills through his entire body. He also tripped and began to fall – right toward the empty elevator shaft.

Thankfully, the elevator door was not actually open. Unfortunately, Jonathan rammed his head into the closed door, sending sparks of pain through his head and neck. After dropping to the ground, he turned to see Ruth walking back to his room, 4450. More curious than anything, Jonathan followed.

Arriving back in his room, he found his geometry notes shredded, blown across the room like a paper confetti snowfall. At the other side of the room was Ruth, hovering up on his desk that faced the window. The curtains were blowing wildly to each side like fluttering wings. She was facing out, gazing down at the ground below.

Jonathan became horrified as he watched Ruth fall out the window. He ran to the ledge and looked down, not finding anything below. He didn't really expect to. After all, she was a ghost. Still, it saddened Jonathan to think that at some point years ago, Ruth did in fact jump.

He stared down at the ground, wondering where she landed, and why she would have jumped. Thoughts traveled back to the baby taken by the shadowy figure down the elevator shaft. *Was that true too?* Jonathan hoped not.

Needless to say, Jonathan's studying did not go well, and the geometry test results didn't go well either. But he was fine with that. He was just glad to graduate and get away from room 4450 and the ghost of Ruth.

History:

Winona State University has been around since 1858, currently enrolling over 8,000 students. Two buildings, Lourdes Hall and Richards Hall, have been known to have paranormal activity.

In Richards Hall, a room is haunted by the ghost of a student who sadly hung himself in a closet back in 1978. His ghost is now seen brushing past residents during the day, or walking aimlessly around at night. Other students claim to see the outline of a human going to and from the showers in the early hours of the morning on the second floor.

Lourdes Hall appears to have most of the strange activity, mainly on the third and fourth floors.

On the third floor of Lourdes Hall, things on the wall have been known to be moved or turned around. Pictures are knocked over, and doors can mysteriously close and lock by themselves. Students will occasionally hear voices out in the hallway, yet when they go to open the door and look, nobody is there.

On the fourth floor of Lourdes Hall, the ghost of Ruth is said to wander about. In particular, she visits room 4450 where she apparently lived back in the 1800s. Footsteps can be heard in the hallway late at night, even when nobody is there. A terrible chill can be found traveling through the air. On rare occasions, the ghost of Ruth has been known to talk with students. It makes me wonder what a ghost would say to me if I were a student there. Better yet, what would I say to the ghost?

Apparently Ruth was a nurse going to college, back when Lourdes Hall was the dormitory in conjunction with St. Theresa's college. Legend has it Ruth got pregnant by a priest.

When the baby was born, the priest who was the father became fearful of what others would think, or of him being kicked out of the priesthood. In a fit of insanity, he grabbed the baby from Ruth and threw it down the elevator shaft. Ruth was terribly distressed and threw herself down the third-north stairwell. Other reports indicate she may have jumped out her window in room 4450.

As the weeks went on, the priest became distressed, not wanting to live with his own actions. He ended up hanging himself where the Lourdes pool is located. Swimmers in the pool area claim to see a body hanging high above them, and have occasionally felt a mysterious tug at their feet while swimming in the water.

Phelps Hall is another building on campus that has some possible paranormal activity. Once in awhile, students will hear children crying. One night in 2003, a custodian specifically heard the cries of children on the third floor. Apparently, the building was used as a day-care center for children back in the 1970s. There was a terrible fire during that time, killing several children. The custodian no longer works alone at night.

Even the Performing Arts Center has its own ghost. Supposedly, a former student of WSU was found unconscious on the floor of the main stage area, after falling from the fly gallery sometime during the evening. He eventually died later of internal injuries. To this day, the area of the stage where the student died is the only section of the roof that doesn't leak, and never has any wasps or bees on it. The lighting system also has mysterious problems, with the switches always being moved to a particular preset mode. And unexplainable sudden chilling rushes of air can be felt. Sometimes, something also can be seen at the end of the long dark hallways at the Performing Arts Center.

Chapter 16
Dead Man's Bridge

"...he could hear something underneath, as if something heavy was swinging from a rope."

Location: Rochester, MN

"We'll see you in the morning," said Daniel to his two friends Bobby and Jimmy, then added, "dead or alive! Ha-ha-ha!"

Both Bobby and Jimmy tried to laugh too, but they were the ones being left behind. The rest of their friends had already been initiated into the gang. Most of them had slept in cemeteries, but Bobby and Jimmy wanted something better—to prove how tough they were. That's when they came up with the idea of sleeping overnight underneath Dead Man's Bridge at Quarry Hill.

Daniel said with a grin, "You guys aren't gonna last a minute up here in Quarry Hill, not with the dead man walking around at night. I've heard about it. Gives me the chills."

Their other friend, Stevie, cackled loudly. "Yeah—with the sun going down in a few more minutes, it's gonna get real dark. And real spooky."

Bobby tried to act fearless as he stammered, "I—I can do this. I'm not scared."

Jimmy could only nod, worried that they would see his teeth chattering.

Daniel left Bobby and Jimmy down underneath the bridge and climbed up on top. Stevie quickly followed. "Ooooooh!" moaned Daniel from above, as if a ghost were floating around. He ended with a classic "Boo!"

"Knock it off!" yelled Bobby. "Just leave us alone. We'll see you in the morning."

"Dead," said Daniel with a ghastly scream, "or alive! Ha-ha-ha-ha!" Daniel jumped up and down on the bridge, sending twigs and dust down on top of Bobby and Jimmy. "Come on, Stevie, let's get out of here before the dead man gets us!" They ran down the dimly-lit path screaming as if being chased by a ghost.

Jimmy looked down the path from underneath the bridge. He could see the old Insane Asylum cemetery in the distance, with faint shadows from the trees flickering in the nearly setting sun. "I think I'd rather be sleeping down there."

"What's the difference?" asked Bobby.

"We got a better chance to run on the flat ground. I don't think I can outrun the dead man from here."

"Relax," said Bobby, "There's no such thing as ghosts and a dead man walking."

Jimmy curled up into a ball, looking up above at the bridge. "I hope you're right."

The two friends settled down underneath the bridge as the sun set behind the trees, extinguishing any remaining shadows. Their parents thought they were on a sleep over, so there was no problem spending the night. Normally, it would have been pitch black out, but luckily there was a full moon, allowing the boys to see somewhat in the darkness.

Jimmy finally got up the courage to talk about the legend. "So do you believe in the dead man? That he hung himself, right here above us?"

Bobby looked up at the bridge in the moonlight. "It's possible. Definitely could be true. But I don't think there's no ghost floating around. Dead is dead as far as I know."

At that moment, a strong gust of wind came up through the winding path from the cemetery, blowing leaves and dust up into the air. The two of them could hear moaning. Within a few seconds the wind subsided, leaving them in silence to ponder what they had just heard.

"Was—was that the wind?" asked Jimmy nervously.

"Of course it was," replied Bobby in more of a question than a statement. The floorboards on the bridge began to

Dead Man's Bridge at the old State
Hospital for the Insane, now the
location of Quarry Hill Nature Center.

creak, starting on one side, then moving to the opposite side. It sounded as if someone was slowly walking across.

"Bobby? Do—do you hear that?"

"Who's there?" asked Bobby, but there was no response. The creaking stopped, then all of a sudden a big swooshing sound came from just below the bridge, and both of them could faintly see the outline of something hanging right above them.

Jimmy was too petrified to speak or move, let alone breathe.

Bobby, although not sure what to believe, was at least smart enough not to stick around. Some dark shadowy figure was hanging from the bridge. "Come, on," squeaked Bobby. "Let's move to a different spot."

Bobby went up the hill past the bridge, practically pulling Jimmy along. Jimmy kept looking back at the bridge, but could see nothing. But he could hear something underneath, as if something heavy was swinging from a rope. They continued along the path away from the bridge until it split two ways.

"Which way should we go?" asked Jimmy, finally able to speak.

"Let's try the right."

The path led to a pit lined with limestone, probably the foundation and basement of an old building. Over the years, trees had grown from the center, spreading out, making it easier for the two of them to climb down into it. Once settled in, they sat there huddled together, thinking about what had just happened.

Bobby could tell Jimmy was really scared. To relax Jimmy, Bobby said, "Don't worry. We'll be fine up here. I don't know what that was, but I didn't want to hang around and find out. Get it? Hang around?"

Jimmy was not amused.

After a few minutes of rest, cracking and snapping sounds could be heard in the distance, along the path coming from dead man's bridge. They sounded like steps and were getting louder, as if something was coming toward them. Something sounded as though it was being dragged along with the steps.

Bobby initially thought it might be the rope from the dead man, still fixed around its neck.

Jimmy grabbed Bobby by the arm, gripping him hard and whispered, "He's coming! The dead man's coming!"

"Quiet!" said Bobby as he peered into the darkness. He could see nothing, yet the footsteps sounded like something was coming into the pit where they rested. Even Bobby was alarmed, not being sure what it was.

The wind died down and the footsteps stopped, making an eerie silence that chilled the boys to the bone. They noticed a mist or fog had rolled into the foundation area, swirling around something standing in the center. It was a dark figure, about as tall as a man. Something hung from its neck.

The boys, petrified with fright, watched as the ghost stood there and began floating into the air two feet above the ground. It grabbed the rope around its neck and began swinging it in the air, as if trying to lasso the boys. Perhaps it wanted to hang them too from the bridge.

That was it for Bobby. He had seen enough. Leaping up from their resting spot he yelled to Jimmy. "Come on! Let's get out of here!"

They clawed their way up the opposite side of the foundation and pulled themselves over the edge. Unfortunately, there was nothing but hillside there, and they ended up rolling down the hill, bouncing off tree trunks and rolling over bushes like a ball in a pinball machine. After tumbling for at least fifty yards, they dropped off a small cliff about eight feet high.

"Ohhh!" said Jimmy, who had fallen on top of Bobby, "That hurt!"

"Well, at least you had a soft landing on me," said Bobby. He got up, brushed himself off and looked around. The boys quickly realized they have fallen down the hill to the front entrance of the caves.

The caves always spooked Jimmy; he never knew what might be lurking in them, either dead or alive. "I don't like the caves—let's move away from here."

Bobby nodded. "Right, let's head for our bikes at the park and get home. I don't care about the stupid gang. Bumping into ghosts is not worth it."

As they turned to leave, a rush of chilling air blew out of the cave entrance. They looked into the cave, and saw a bright light coming from within. Seconds later, they heard wheels turning, and a white, ghostly wagon, full of food and boxes coming out of the cave. Both boys jumped aside as the wagon continued out of the cave right through the iron bars, floating down the path before vanishing into the forest.

Not needing to be prodded, Jimmy ran. Bobby followed, trying to keep up. He had never seen Jimmy run that fast. The two boys ran around the west side of Quarry Hill, right between the Insane Asylum cemetery and down below dead man's bridge.

"Jimmy! Watch out for the drop off!" It was too late, Jimmy turned the corner too fast, and ended up rolling down a steep incline off the side of the path.

Bobby looked down over the hill at Jimmy; he was lying there about thirteen feet below. "Hold on, I'm coming."

Carefully climbing down the steep incline, Bobby managed to get to Jimmy. That's when he noticed the other cave, and the lights coming from within.

"Boy, does my head hurt!" said Jimmy, groggy from his fall.

"Jimmy," said Bobby, who was looking straight into the small cave. He could start to see ghostly faces in there, all of them marching toward the entrance where they lay. Apparently, there was more to worry about than just one dead man. There were hundreds of ghosts coming toward them.

"I think I hurt my arm," said Jimmy, still not seeing the brigade of ghostly souls.

"Jimmy, I think we gotta go, or there may be more hurt than just your arm."

Hundreds of apparitions were now marching to the front of the cave; Bobby pulled Jimmy up and helped him down the hillside to the cemetery. "Don't look back," said Bobby, who noticed that the ghosts were following them out of the cave and down through the cemetery.

The two boys finally reached their bikes at the edge of the park and frantically unlocked them, all the time hoping that the apparitions would not follow them further. As they hopped on their bikes to peddle away, they looked back one last time at the cemetery, but saw nothing in the moonlit night. The memories of that night, however, would never disappear. Years later they still talked about the night under dead man's bridge—nobody believed them, but then nobody wanted to find out on their own.

History:

The Dead Man's Bridge tale above is based on reports of strange occurrences happening at what is now Quarry Hill Park and Nature Center, located in Northwest Rochester. Rumor has it, an unknown individual hung himself from the bridge back in the late 1960s. But there are many more reasons why the place is haunted.

Historically, Quarry Hill started as a State Hospital (known as an Insane Asylum) back in the 1870s. Thousands of patients visited the hospital, and unfortunately thousands died there. The cemetery on the premise was used from 1886 to 1965, and 2,019 people are buried there (most are in unmarked graves—although there is a recent project in place to provide tombstones for most of them). The State Hospital itself closed in 1965, and the 212-acre land was purchased from the state by the City of Rochester.

In the 1880s, the property was also used as a quarry, mostly crushing limestone rock for gravel roads. At one point, it contained the largest stone-crushing machine in Minnesota. They eventually closed the quarry in 1950.

The caves on the premise were excavated by Thomas Coyne and other workers in 1882, and were primarily used to store food and supplies for the state hospital. Wagons used to cart food in and out of the caves, and on tours of the cave, you can still see the wagon wheel hub marks. (They are still giving tours I believe on last Sunday of each month.) The

hospital used the caves until the 1940s, at which time they abandoned them due to the hospital using refrigeration units instead.

In 1972, the City of Rochester began work on creating the Quarry Hill Park and Nature Center. Over the next thirty years, the city built a nature center building, paths were paved, a large pond was excavated, and now over a million people have visited the center.

In doing my research, I spent some time trying to find out if there were any police records recording a death by hanging on the bridge around the 1960s. I could not find any evidence of it. Still, there are records dating back to the late mid 1860s of over 2,000 mentally ill patients and workers dying on the premise. There are ample reasons for the location to have wandering spirits with many people being killed at the asylum or tragically dying of disease back then.

One of several caves at Quarry Hill Nature Center, reported to have restless spirits inside late at night.

The cemetery for the old State Hospital of the Insane. Several thousand are buried in unmarked graves across the open field.

Field Trip:

For my field trip, I stopped by the park with my handy dandy digital audio recorder, a.k.a. D.A.R.R.E.N. (Digital Audio Recorder for Really Eerie Noises). I started over on the northwest side by the cemetery, figuring I might as well cut to the chase and check it out. I'd been to Quarry Hill Park many times before, touring the caves as well, so this field trip would be nothing new to me.

I'm afraid I was correct, nothing was new, other than the cemetery had some workers putting in new tombstones. One by one they were laying them in the ground—all in the correct location, based on old cemetery lot maps. In talking with the supervisor, it turns out there are 2,019 graves. You wouldn't know that by walking around. There were only a couple dozen graves marked prior to their work. Now, depending on funding, they will eventually have all 2,019 graves marked.

As I walked around the cemetery with my recorder, I captured nothing unusual, except a few zaps and crackles, which could be normal electrical interference—although there were no power lines nearby, and I would think none buried in the cemetery. Interestingly enough, I noticed the zapping occurred whenever we talked about a particular grave, stating the name of one of the deceased.

I took a walk up the hill and found one of the caves just up from the cemetery. It had bars on the front, so you could not walk inside. I took a couple pictures, and the results initially freaked me out. The walls and ceilings were covered in dark red colors, like blood. No doubt it was from the natural limestone and iron oxides leaching out, but it still looked very creepy, as if blood had been splattered everywhere. The other interesting thing was that this cave (one of several in the park) looked like it may have once gone back further. I couldn't quite tell, as it

Another small cave gated up, to keep us from going in, or possibly to make sure something doesn't get out.

was dark and I hadn't brought a flashlight. Perhaps this was one of the closed-off caves rumored to populate the quarry.

From the entrance of the cave, I walked farther up to the quarry (the quarry is in the center of a huge hill, more like a foothill to a mountain). I found a path at the top and followed it to the right. At some point I took a wrong turn, but ended up in the basement/foundation of an old building. I had been up there dozens of times before, but had never noticed it. I climbed down into the foundation and looked around. Most of it was filled with dirt and trees, and I found nothing unusual about it.

Next, I walked north to Dead Man's Bridge. I approached it and took my first picture of it. Strangely enough, the picture had that eerie ectoplasm look to it, as if a ghost had materialized in it, sending splashes of white phantom gook everywhere. Freaky indeed. But I'm sure it was caused by my camera being set incorrectly (although I'm not sure how that happened). The rest of the pictures I took came out normal.

I crawled down underneath the bridge and took more pictures, and walked back and forth around the area. It really didn't feel that creepy. The only weird thing was that I noticed one of the floorboards underneath had some dark oozing liquid dripping from it. It hadn't rained in weeks, so I wondered why that board, in the center of the bridge, was wet. And it wasn't wet from the top, only from underneath.

As I walked across the bridge one last time, I noticed someone had etched the words, 'dead man's bridge' on it. Obviously someone else had heard of the tale. I also saw the initials G.G.G. engraved on one of the floorboards. Could it be the initials of the man who hung himself? Possibly, but more likely some gang member's initials from the neighborhood. Although maybe that's the gang that tried to stay overnight underneath the bridge.

I walked through the quarry, investigating the other crumbling foundations and outdoor fireplaces. Nothing seemed strange to me. Only when I made it to the cave entrance did

I feel a bit spooked. Especially when a strong gust of chilling air blew at me from within the cave. Of course you would expect that, since your typical cave has a temperature of only 65 degrees inside it.

A locked iron gate blocked the entrance to the caves. I had been in there many times before, and it was always fun and exciting. Never any thoughts of ghosts, but there were plenty of bats to be found.

Overall, I'd say that Quarry Hill certainly has the potential to be haunted. It's a great place to spend the afternoon however, walking around the quarry, looking for fossils, and exploring the caves. Still, I'm not sure if I would spend a night there…

Chapter 17
Demonic Hellhound

"We quickly realized that we were not alone as something in the dark distance was snapping twigs and shrubs as it moved."

Wooded area of Forestville State Park, possible home of the Demonic Hellhound.

Location: Forestville State Park

used to enjoy camping, getting out to see the great outdoors. But ever since my run in with what I call a demonic hellhound, with its glowing red eyes and tarnished pointy fangs, well, now I do all my camping at a Best Western…

I called up my best friend from high school, Jeff, to see if he wanted to do some camping on the weekend. Both of us had gone off to college and had not seen each other for over a month.

"Great! Thanks, Tom, for asking. This weekend works fine. Where should we go?" Jeff sounded eager to do some serious camping, not that we were that hardcore with it, but the few times we've gone it had been enjoyable.

"Forestville State Park," I replied. "It's about thirty minutes east of where we grew up in Austin. They have some hiking trails and an old cave to explore."

"Sounds like fun. Would you believe I'm still packed from the last trip? Not sure how stinky the rain gear is, or the tent."

We had camped out at Nerstrand Park during the summer, which turned out to be a disaster. It had rained the entire weekend. If his stuff was still packed, it would probably be very smelly. Moldy, too. "Don't worry about the packing. Just grab the essentials. I have my parents' camper this time. Should be tons of fun."

On Friday afternoon Jeff met me at my parents' house. I was busy hitching up the camper to my Jeep when he pulled into the driveway. My parents had gone south already for the winter, even though it was only September. I wondered when the Minnesota cold would get to me, turning me into a snowbird and traveling south to the warm weather each year. I got up and waved to Jeff, coming over to shake his hand. "Jeff. Great to see you again. Go ahead and throw your gear inside while I finish with the hitch."

Jeff climbed inside the camper, and a moment later I heard him yell, "Ahhh!"

The scream startled me, making my hand slip on the wheel crank for the hitch, slamming my hand into the sharp metal frame. "Ahhh!" I echoed back to Jeff from the pain, angry because of my now chewed up knuckles with blood. Jeff came bolting out of the camper and threw something at me. I instinctively caught the thing, and then dropped it as I realize it was a dead rat. A real big one, too. And big-time stinky.

Jeff laughed. "What the heck are your parents doing with a dead rat in the fridge? And boy, does it reek in there."

"Not sure," I said, staring at the rat's lifeless whiskers and yellowed buckteeth. "Must have crawled in and died."

Jeff kicked the rat in front of me while covering his nose, "You got that right. That thing stinks."

I tossed the rat in a bag and threw it in the garbage.

With the sun dropping close to the horizon, we hopped in my Jeep and headed for the park. Most of our talk centered around our experiences with the first month of college; I had gone to Minnesota State Mankato, Jeff had gone east to University of Eau Claire, Wisconsin. Both of our experiences were similar, about the serious studying needed, the major house parties, and the fantastic looking girls everywhere you turned. But we both agreed that even with all the exciting changes in our lives, it was great to be back home for a while, and hang out with old friends.

"Hey," said Jeff, "I see the entrance to the park up ahead."

We pulled into the Ranger Station on the right to check in. The parking lot wasn't full, which meant there wouldn't be very many campers. Of course, not too many want to camp in the cold month of October. But we had the camper complete with heater, so we'd stay plenty warm.

The Park Ranger finished checking us in and gave us our permit. He looked at us and said, "No parties, right? And quiet time is 10 P.M."

Although we did bring a case of Schmidt beer, we had no plans of making this trip a drunk fest. I nodded to the Park Ranger in agreement that we would be quiet. I only wish the demonic hellhound would have obeyed the ranger's request.

The Park Ranger then added, "Oh, and one last thing. There's a bear in the forest, so be careful where you leave your food."

Jeff and I looked at each other, surprised. There had not been a bear sighted in Southeastern Minnesota for years.

The Park Ranger saw our expression of shock and added, "A family camping two weekends ago heard something foraging in the woods around midnight. Gave them quite the scare, especially when it entered their campsite and began smashing their cooler and camping chairs."

I gulped and asked, "Was anyone in the family hurt?"

Park Ranger laughed and said, "Absolutely not. Mom and Dad grabbed the kids and hopped in the car. Within seconds they were out of there." He could see we were bothered by the story and added, "Don't worry about the bear, or whatever it was. Just keep your food in your camper, or high up on a rope in a tree."

"Thanks," I said, not too sure about camping with a bear around. Of course, I knew bears were just as scared of humans as we were of them. Rattling some pans would do the trick, unless it was a grisly bear. In worst case, we could play dead. As long as it was 'play' dead, and not 'real' dead.

Jeff and I pulled into the campgrounds, searching for our campsite, lucky number 13. We weren't too pleased with the number assignment, but neither of us were superstitious. After a long winding road, we found a sign directing us further into the woods for the campsites 10 through 15. Several minutes passed before we finally arrived at the site. No other campers were at the other campsites, and since it was dark already, we doubted any others would show up.

Within only a few minutes, we had unhitched the camper and started a blazing campfire. We sat back peacefully sitting in our chairs, drinking a few beers, absorbing the cool breeze and woodsy smell of the damp forest floor.

Our rest didn't last long. We quickly realized that we were not alone as something in the dark distance was snapping twigs and shrubs as it moved.

We both turned to look at where the noise was coming from. Thoughts of a wild bear leaping out of the woods made me nervous. I grabbed my whittling knife, ready for action.

Jeff laughed. "Like your knife will help save us from a bear! But I doubt there's any bears around here."

I put my knife away as the sounds of shrubs moving dissipated. "You're right. I'd be better off shoving my arm down the bear's throat."

We both laughed at that, when suddenly something jumped out of the darkness, landing on top of our fire and sending a huge flurry of flame and ash into the air. We jumped back fast, not wanting it to burn us.

"What the heck was that?" said Jeff as he fell backward in his chair.

I looked in the fire to see what it was and couldn't believe it. "It's a rat. Another one of those dead rats."

"Whew!" said Jeff. "Yeah, now I smell it. It's worse barbecued like that. Get that thing off the fire!"

After several attempts, we were able to flick the dead rat off. We threw it in a bag over to the side of our campsite. But no sooner had we sat down to enjoy another beer when more shrubs were moving and twigs snapping somewhere out in the darkness. It was apparently going to be a busy night.

This time both of us instinctively took out our whittling knifes, not at all wanting another dead rat thrown at us. I looked into the dark shadows beyond the campfire as I told Jeff, "It has to be some kids playing around with us."

Jeff said, "Yeah, I think so." He turned and yelled toward the rustling in the darkness. "Whoever you are, stop throwing the dead rats!" Then he added as he looked at his watch, "It's past quiet time, and I've also got a knife."

At that same moment, something once again flew at them, but this time it smacked Jeff right in the face, sending him falling backward. Unfortunately, the fire was also behind him. He landed right in the fire. I don't know how, but he didn't seem to get burned. Sure, his pants were smoldering a bit, and the other dead rat thrown at him was burning just fine, but Jeff wasn't.

"That was weird," I said as I helped Jeff out of the fire.

Jeff didn't say anything, too stunned with the thought of almost being barbecued.

We decided to search the area with our flashlights for whoever was causing the pranks. After twenty minutes we found no one. With the desire to sit around the campfire gone, we decided to head into the camper and play some cards. Jeff put out the fire and I went to get rid of the two dead rats. But they were both gone.

"That's odd, where'd the bag of rats go?" I asked.

"Beats me. They should be right over there. Maybe the bear took them back," said Jeff with a chuckle.

We settled into the camper, cracking open a couple more beers and setting the poker chips out to be counted. Several games of poker played on, with Jeff seeming to be the lucky one. After an hour of playing, he was up twenty bucks.

Smiling, Jeff said, "This must be my lucky day."

At that moment we heard a horrific snarling noise right outside the camper, followed by a jolt that nearly flipped it on its side.

"What the—" was all I could say before several more thumps hit the camper. Wham! Wham! Wham! There was a hideous snarling noise, as if a humongous rabid dog were standing outside our front door.

Then I saw it. I looked out the window to see two crimson eyes staring into the window. I could also see drooling sharp fangs, big ones, pointing out of this creature's long snout.

"It's the bear!" yelled Jeff, who had not looked out the window at what I saw. I knew it wasn't a bear. Then again, I didn't know what it was. But it howled like a wolf.

I turned to Jeff and said, "Does a bear howl?"

"Then what is it?"

"Don't know. And I don't want to find out."

Now the camper was rocking back and forth, with each side raising several feet off the ground. This creature was powerful. Just then, the door to the fridge opened up, and the bag of burnt rats fell out.

"How did they get in there?" asked Jeff as he tumbled back and forth.

"Beats me," I replied. For some reason I had this idea that the strange hellish dog beast outside wanted the rats. It didn't make any sense to me, but I knew what to do. "Throw them out the door," I yelled to Jeff.

Jeff looked at the door, then back at me. "I'm not opening the door. What if that thing comes in here?"

The camper was really rocking now. Several times it nearly flipped completely sideways. I held onto the bathroom door and yelled, "In a few more seconds, I think that thing will be in anyway!"

That was enough for Jeff. He pulled and pushed his way over to the door with the bag of burned rats, opened the door and threw them out. As he went to close the door, the creature stuck its head into the camper. Its glowing red eyes stared at both of us for a second, and drool from its sharp fangs dropped to the steps. The creature then reached up at Jeff's wrist, slicing it open with one of its claws. "Rats!" yelled the creature in a raspy voice.

"Ahhh!" yelled Jeff as blood began to drip from his wrist.

As Jeff fell to the ground in shock, the creature turned to look at me. I looked around for a weapon to protect us with. The only thing I could find as I fell back into the bathroom was a toilet scrubby brush. Now I can tell you one thing, I'm not at all ashamed to have beaten down this Hellhound thing with a toilet scrubby, cause that's what I did. I think the chemicals (or other smells) scared the thing off. As soon as I swatted the thing on the nose with the nylon bristles, it turned and fled. It grabbed the bag of dead rats too. I never found out anything more about the rats either; I was just glad to get rid of them.

I looked at Jeff's wrist. It wasn't cut too deep, but it was bleeding enough to make a mess out of the carpet in the camper. "We need to get you to the hospital," I said.

"Sounds good to me," said Jeff. "Anything to get away from this place."

I helped Jeff into the Jeep and I went back to hitch up the camper. Or at least that was what I planned. But the Hellhound came back. I don't know, but I think he was mad about the toilet scrubby. I wasn't going to wait around to tell it I was sorry. I dropped my tools near the hitch as the creature came running at me. Thankfully, I had the door open on the Jeep so I jumped in.

I trembled with the keys, dropping them several times to the floor. When I finally got the key in the ignition I looked and saw two things. First was Jeff, who had turned white and I think was in severe shock. Secondly, I saw why he was in shock. The Hellhound creature was standing in front of the car. It must have been eight feet tall, all hunched over and hairy from head to toe.

I slammed the key further into the ignition and started the car. The noise startled the Hellhound for a moment, but then it jumped. At first we didn't know where it went; it was as if it jumped straight up into the air. But we weren't about to get out and look for it. I shifted my Jeep into drive and tore out of the campsite. We had made it all the way to the parking lot before realizing where the Hellhound ended up. It was on top of the Jeep.

The creature looked down at me from the windshield. Instinctively, I slammed on the breaks. This sent the Hellhound creature flying out in front of the Jeep. As I saw it tumble several times, I panicked and began driving again, running over the creature with a thump-thump.

I ended up taking Jeff straight to the hospital in Austin where he received eight stitches to his wrist. We didn't bother trying to explain how he got the cut—nobody would believe us. But as the years fly by, I find myself thinking more about the Hellhound, how lucky we were to escape. I was glad we got away, and didn't want that thing terrorizing anyone else. So maybe telling a few people wouldn't hurt.

Just to let you know, Jeff and I never went camping again. And my parents were not at all happy with the camper. It was bashed in pretty good, and Jeff's blood was impossible to get out of the carpet. Of course the smell was the worst. That dead rat smell never went away, no matter how many times we cleaned it.

History:

The source of this story came from two young men that claim to have been terrorized by some strange creature one night while camping in Southeast Minnesota. As the story goes, the two of them were camping somewhere about fifteen miles from the Iowa border. That could mean the incident happened in a number of places. But based on looking at the map, the most likely candidate would be Forestville State Park.

The park itself is pretty secluded, along with the campsites. Although I would think that for this to occur, there would be many eyewitnesses, or tat least someone else hearing the sounds of the camper being beaten up. The likelihood of having some evil possessed monster dog living in the park is unlikely. Southeastern Minnesota in general is not that desolate; it's not as if you can drive for a hundred miles and still not see signs of civilization. Sure, I'll admit you could get lost in Forestville State Park, but not for long. It's not more than a several hours hike from one side to the other, although if you were disoriented, you could circle around for quite some time. But having a wild Hellhound on the loose is just not probable in my opinion. Furthermore, you would have most likely had other incidents show up, of which I found none.

If in fact something attacked the campers, I would have to agree that what they found was most likely a large bear. But even that is highly unlikely, as there hasn't been a bear found in Southeastern Minnesota in many years. Of course, this story could have been from decades ago, too.

Field Trip:

I've camped many times in Southeastern Minnesota, and although it can get somewhat spooky out late at night, I've never heard of any strange creatures attacking campers. Although just recently there was an attack up north in Itasca State Park, weeks before we were headed up for a Boy Scout campout.

Needless to say, there were several stories on that trip about spooky animals lurking near your tent while you slept.

Stopping in at Forestville State Park is like any other Minnesota State Park, at least for the parks in Central and Southern Minnesota. It has a quiet camping area for your tent or camper, and has some great woods for hiking. With my digital recorder running, I walked through the area, trying to see if there were any restless spirits lingering. I found myself enjoying the walk around; it was very peaceful and relaxing. No bears or hellhounds to be found. Later investigation of the digital records did not reveal any EVPs.

I'm working with a Boy Scout Troop that's thinking of going camping at Forestville State Park perhaps next year. I'm not sure if I'll mention the story about this Hellhound, though. They may not want to go then. Or perhaps it would be exciting, making them want to camp there even more. You never know. But I know for sure it would make a great story to tell around the flickering campfire. I just hope it doesn't come true while we're there.

Chapter 18
Ghost in the Pew

*"You'd be sitting in the pew praying away for good things to happen,
when all of a sudden you'd hear whispering voices."*

Vang Church in Dennison, where parishioners have more than just themselves sitting in the pews.

Location: Dennison

’ve been a member of the church for over six decades
and have seen a few strange things happen that I
can't explain…

First off, I'm a God-fearing man at the young age of
eighty-two. There are a lot of things that have gone through
my head, some good and some not so good. Some of it
spooky, too. I'm not sure if all the ghost stories coming from

the church are real. I can only testify to what I've seen. And there is a lot of that.

There's this picture floating around from the 1930s. I was around back then, but just a boy. I wasn't living in Dennison then either, but I remember first seeing the picture back in the 1950s. I shrugged the picture off at first, thinking it was some type of photographic illusion or trickery. It has this fuzzy picture of a man, or woman perhaps. It was hard to tell. But it looked like it was hovering in the church, on its way down into the basement. Just like a ghost.

Now the story could have ended there, but it didn't. Turns out the ghostly picture was real. I know because I've seen the ghost, years later in the 70s. I was in the church late at night, doing some extra prayers for my son who at the time had a fierce cold, pneumonia I believe. I was busy giving thanks to the Lord with my head bowed low into the pews. But then I heard something up near the altar.

I knew I was the only one in the church; the pastor had left at least an hour before. At first I thought it might be another member of the church, coming in for prayer too. But what I saw wasn't no person. At least I've never seen anybody walking like that. Actually, it was more like floating. Three feet off the ground. A ghostly white figure too, sort of see-through.

I stared in disbelief as the thing hovered in front of the altar for a few seconds, like it was giving thanks itself or something. I'm not sure how ghosts work, if they need to pray as well. I suppose they do, maybe that's how they get out of where they're stuck and on to heaven. I watched the ghostly thing as it turned and floated over to the basement door on the side of the church. I thought it was going to bump into a door, or a wall, but it didn't. It went right through. That's when I decided I had done enough praying and headed home.

Over the years, other strange things have happened, mostly voices. You'd be sitting in the pew praying away for good things to happen, when all of a sudden you'd hear whispering voices. Sometimes I've been there with several parishioners, and all of us could hear them. Can't really make out what they're saying, but it doesn't matter. It's spooky no matter what they'd be saying.

The other thing that usually happens is with stuff disappearing and reappearing somewhere else. Mostly pens, papers, keys—all sorts of small items. You'd swear (although not in God's house) that you left your keys in your jacket pocket on a hanger in the church entryway. But when it came time to leave, you'd find your keys on a shelf nearby.

Now I have a great fear of God, but the ghosts don't bother me. I suppose they have as much right as I do to roam the planet. Although I'm not too keen about going down into the basement of the church late at night. There's no telling what sort of ghost I'll meet down there, or if I'll pass the ghost on the way back up.

History:

The Vang Church was originally built over 170 years ago in the small town of Dennison just south of Northfield. Back then the town was thriving, complete with a hotel, blacksmith, wagon shop, shoemaker, and physician. But by the 1880s and 1890s, the town all but dried up. Most likely due to transportation, with the towns that had trains going through them growing.

At some point along the way the church had become haunted. Numerous reports of activity have been described over the years, and in the 1930s, a picture of a ghost was taken. It was of a blurry apparition, crossing the church to the basement steps. One could easily dismiss the photo as a fake, or a trick of the shadows. Still others claim it is real.

Several church members have seen the picture, as well as other mysterious ghostly sightings, but nobody can determine who the ghost is. Perhaps it is a pastor from a previous congregation, wandering around the church that he loved all his life. Or maybe it is an organist, walking through the pews on his way to play one last concerto.

Strange voices can also be heard throughout the church. Several parishioners claim to hear voices from places in the church when nobody is there. Even faint whispers of singing can be found in the silence late at night.

It seems as though there is obviously some type of haunting going on. However, to fortify the claim, a paranormal investigation team needs to spend some time there. Perhaps a few video cameras and voice recorders will pull the ghost out of hiding, capturing its presence on tape. Then once and for all we can agree that Vang Church has got more in its congregation than just people.

Chapter 19

Haunted Mansion

"...I won't go down near the boathouse area."

Location: Rochester

'll never forget the tour I had at the Mayowood Mansion. Some say the place is haunted and I now believe they are correct.

Visiting Rochester, Minnesota for a medical checkup at the Mayo Clinic, I decided to take a tour of the city. Upon asking around, I was told that a trip to the Mayowood Mansion was a must. It was the very home that the great Mayo brothers lived in, along with other family members over the years.

Located just a few minutes out of town (way out in the country back when it was built by Dr. Mayo), I drove my car to the front entrance, paid the attendant for the tour, and drove up the long driveway. I was immediately taken back by the sheer grandness of the mansion, with its dozens of steps ascending to the original entrance located at the front of the house.

I drove around to the side and parked my car, thinking of how wonderful it must have been to live there, running through the forest and playing in the numerous bubbling fountains, trickling waterfalls, and ponds built into the hillside. I walked up to the side door, amazed at the size of the mansion, and with forty rooms, wondered what it would have been like to play hide and seek.

After a short video showing the history of Mayowood Mansion, the tour guide took us to the main entrance, which was actually on the side of the house. The front entrance was replaced with large windows after the first few years, presumably due to the Mayos not wanting to shovel snow and ice off all those dozens of steps. From the main entrance on the side, we moved upstairs into the living quarters, with a pipe organ in one room, a library in another, and a multitude of sitting, and family rooms. Large mirrors imported from around the world hung in many of the rooms.

The tour was going along fine until I started to have a heavy, dark feeling, as if someone were watching me from behind. I kept looking back, but there was never anything there. That is until at one point I thought I saw a shadow on the wall move. I looked around to see what might have made the shadow, but I could not determine what it was. The shadow from the corner of my eye danced on the walls several times for me while on the tour.

When we got into the dining hall, I became fixated on all the china and glassware. There were beautifully handcrafted crystal glasses and custom-made plates with the initials C.M. on them, for Charles Mayo. While the majority of the group continued into a large sitting area, I remained for a moment, mesmerized by a tall, crystal candelabra. As I was about to join the rest of the group, I noticed the candelabra move. At first it was like somebody had bumped it. But then it altogether picked up and teetered over to the other side of the table it was resting on. At that same instance, I felt a draft blow through me, chilling me deep under my skin. I gasped at the moving candelabra, and looked around to ask if anyone else saw it, but nobody else was in the room.

The next room was a large sitting area, with life-sized portraits of the Mayo brothers Charles and Joseph. A painting of Edith Mayo also hung on a separate wall. What interested me was in the picture of Joseph Mayo. As I walked around the room, it looked as though his eyes were staring at me, no matter where I walked. That sent chills up and down my spine. Dark wood panels covered the entire room, which added to the darkness of the room.

The tour continued up to the third level where the bedrooms were located. The guide explained that there were five levels in the mansion, with the fourth level a ballroom and fifth an

Mayowood Mansion in Rochester, where tourists have reported seeing strange things occur.

observatory, but both of the top levels were closed to the tour. Our guide continued, explaining the living quarters of the Mayowood mansion, then allowed us to wander around and inspect the rooms. Each room had authentic beds, furniture, and wall coverings from when the Mayo family lived there.

As we walked around, I distinctively heard footsteps above us from the fourth level, even though the guide indicated it was closed off. Furthermore, when I approached the children's playroom, I was startled to see a rocking horse moving slightly on its own. Being that most of the room was roped off, I couldn't figure out how it would be moving. Another tourist popped his head in and saw the horse rocking back and forth, but didn't think anything of it.

The rest of the tour was uneventful, but my walk down through the forest to the boathouse was eerie to say the least. Although everything was dilapidated and run down due to the lack of use, I kept having these visual sensations of the place back the way it was in the late 1950s. Beautifully bubbling water fountains and ponds, and children laughing and playing. But the happiness ended as suddenly as it began. It was replaced by feelings of sadness, the kind you get when someone very close has died.

To this day I can't forget that feeling of loss, of loneliness down near where the boathouse once was. I've been back to Rochester many times for other medical checkups, and I've even toured the mansion again. But I won't go down near the boathouse area. Not so much because of any scary feeling, but because of the sadness I felt while being down there.

History:

The Mayowood Mansion was first built in 1911 by the cofounder of the Mayo Clinic, Dr. Charles H. Mayo (known as Dr. Chuck). Several generations of Mayo have lived in the thirty-eight-room mansion, up until 1965 when the Mayo family donated it to the Olmsted County Historical Society.

In 1970, the estate was listed in the National Register of Historical Places.

Dr. Chuck had a strong love for nature and wildlife, which was one of the reasons for moving out into the country. Of course, now the mansion is pretty much in the city, although forest and a few farm fields still surround it.

The mansion was big enough to have a fourth-level ballroom, where Dr. Chuck would invite guests over for dancing each week. The children could also use it in the winter to ride bikes and roller skate. The fifth level was the top floor, and was really just an observatory for Dr. Charlie's (Charles Mayo Sr.) mother to gaze at the stars.

Many famous guests have stayed or visited at the mansion, including Helen Keller, the King and Queen of Nepal, and past Presidents of the United States.

The conservatory and library area is decorated with large paintings of Charles Mayo (Dr. Chuck), Joseph Mayo, and Edith Mayo. The walls are covered in wood panels, and it turns out the wood came from doors in a Rochester elementary school that had been torn down. Some say Dr. Chuck went to school there and put the doors in his room for nostalgic reasons.

The mansion has many other rooms, including two kitchens, staff sleeping quarters, several dining areas, and even an elevator (supposedly one of the first elevators in the region). One could easily spend hours exploring the dozens of rooms and the multitude of original artifacts and furniture from when the mansion was once inhabited by the Mayo family.

There is a ton of more information I could describe about the location, including the various houses built nearby and the farm down the road. At one point Dr. Chuck had a couple thousand acres set aside for farming and wildlife. Over the decades Rochester became synonymous with Mayo. And it all started back in the mid 1800s with a tornado and Franciscan Sisters treating the wounded. From there, the Mayo Empire began, with a multitude of buildings now sprawled out across the Rochester area.

Field Trip:

I decided to take a tour of the Mayowood mansion and see for myself what kind of spooky things might be happening. Although they did not allow cameras on the tour, audio equipment (for taking notes) was acceptable. That meant D.A.R.R.E.N., my Digital Audio Recorder of Really Eerie Noises came along.

We started in the old garage with a video of the Mayowood history. From there we went into the main entrance area, and up to the main living quarters. I continued on with the tour, walking through various rooms. It wasn't until we reached the old conservatory and library room that some interesting things began to occur.

First off all, the paintings in the room spooked me. In particular, a large painting of Dr. Joseph Graham Mayo. It was weird how it seemed to be looking at you from anywhere in the room. Furthermore, I captured some apparent EVP, or Electronic Voice Phenomenon, while walking near the painting of Dr. Joseph. In later analysis, I heard a voice whisper something like, 'deny it'. I have no clue what it means, but it didn't matter to me. Just having a voice show up out of nowhere was creepy enough.

The other startling event at the same time was with a middle-aged woman who started getting dizzy. We had to pause the tour, right in front of the painting of Joseph Mayo. I decided to walk nearby the painting, asking if the spirit of Joseph Mayo were here. To my surprise, I received another EVP that clearly whispered, 'yes'. And when the tour guide mentions Dr. Joe, the recording skips, or repeats itself. Very odd indeed.

As it turns out, I learned through my research how Dr. Joseph Mayo died. He was tragically killed in a car-train accident near the town of Alma, Wisconsin, on November 9, 1936. Interestingly enough, one fact of the accident was held from reporters: Foosie, Dr. Joe's dog, was in the car with him the night of the accident, and an autopsy reported a bullet wound to the dog's head. It seems that Dr. Joe might have won a large sum of money playing poker that night, and accusations circled that Dr. Joe had possibly been murdered. Perhaps that's why the words, 'deny it' showed up on my EVP. Maybe Dr. Joseph himself is trying to tell us to deny that his death was an accident.

Furthermore, Dr. Joe's wife, Ruth, was devastated by the loss, and ended up killing herself a few years later with a gunshot wound to the head. As one could imagine, if any hauntings occur at the Mayowood mansion, it could certainly involve Dr. Joe and Ruth.

The remaining tour was uneventful, other than the occasional chilly draft, which could be attributed to poor ventilation. Although the tour took place in the summer with 90-degree weather outside, so I'm not too sure where the cold drafts came from.

Outside the mansion, I walked around the perimeter, taking pictures (with permission) and recording any possible EVP. No EVPs occurred, yet I did capture a couple possible orbs. These are circle-like entities of energy captured in pictures and video. A couple of them were most likely caused by glare from the sun, but on the shaded side of the house I still captured them. Since it was shaded, I'm not sure how there could have been any glare, but it's still a possibility.

As far as the boathouse area, I did not feel anything sad or depressing down there, other than that it's sad that the place is in ruins. Over the decades, the area down by the lake has crumbled into nothing but piles of rubble and overgrown shrubs and trees—although I'm sure the Olmsted Historical Society plans on returning the place to its original glory, provided the appropriate funds come in.

In the end, my recommendation is to take the tour yourself and see what you find. I definitely felt some creepy spots in the mansion, and can't explain the EVP on the recorder, and the orbs don't make sense either. Still, with the tragedy of Dr. Joe and Ruth, there is certainly the potential for paranormal activity, not to mention the sheer energy of all the prominent figures visiting the site over the decades. All of that powerful energy might possibly wake up the spirits of Mayowood and give you goose bumps on your tour through the mansion.

Chapter 20
Haunted Travois

"His eyes really scared me. They were dark red, almost glowing in the morning light."

Root River Trail in Lanesboro, where joggers supposedly see spirits along the path early in the morning.

Location: Lanesboro

The Root River Trail in Lanesboro is a great place to ride your bike, or take a long hike on its miles of paved paths. That is of course if you like ghosts…

I'm a fitness junky. I'll admit it. There's nothing like a good jog at 6 A.M. in the morning, just about the time when the sun rises for the day. And nothing wimpy, we're talking ten miles every morning. My favorite place to exercise used to be along the Root River Trail down in Lanesboro. I say 'used to', because I won't go back there—not in the morning at least. Too scary for me. Every time I think about taking an early morning jog in Lanesboro, I see the glowing eyes of that ghost, a Native American spirit running at me, with a full-feathered headdress and waving a tomahawk.

Kirby never minded the walks. That's because he's a greyhound dog. They love to run. The ghost issue happened on a Monday morning in October, starting out the same as all the other days. Kirby was anxious to get going, unfortunately, he would have to wait the twenty-minute drive from Chatfield were we lived. But things felt a little different that morning. Not spooky, just different. Even Kirby noticed something. He was not his usual self, acting kind of timid and quiet as we got closer to Lanesboro.

As I pulled into the parking lot near the trail, I could definitely tell something was wrong. There was the smell of electricity in the air, the kind you have during an electrical storm. But there weren't any clouds in the sky. The other thing odd was how still the air was. Not a single leaf on any of the trees were moving. What made matters worse was that Kirby wouldn't come out of the car.

"Come on, Kirby!" I said enthusiastically. "Walkies time!" I had rations for moments like this. Scooby Snacks—just like the ones on TV. Kirby loved them. "Here ya go!" I said as I threw one out away from the car. He still didn't move. I threw another, and then another. Finally, the temptation of multiple Scooby Snacks was too much. He jumped out of the car as I closed the door behind him. Though Kirby thoroughly enjoyed the treats, he was not at all happy with me tricking him.

We began our jog like any other early morning, briskly passing underneath the archway of trees as we pounded the pavement further into the woods. Since the trail was an old railroad train bed, the jog was smooth and relaxing. I was always surprised why there was so very few that used the path in the morning. It was a great way to wake up.

Except for this morning, Kirby was not cooperating. We reached the crest of a small hill when Kirby decided to stop altogether. For some reason, he wouldn't go any further.

"Come on, boy. Time to run!" I had a couple more snacks in my jacket, but even those wouldn't make him move. He thought something was wrong. It didn't take long for me to realize what it was.

In the distance down the trail, I could see something moving. At first I figured it was another jogger, but then I noticed it was much bigger than that. As it got closer, I could tell it was a horse and rider. That by itself was not too unusual, with horse trails scattered around on the main jogging paths. What did seem odd was that the rider was dressed in Native American clothing, with a buckskin shirt and pants, beads across his chest, red paint along his cheeks, and a full-feathered headdress on top.

I thought perhaps there was an old Cowboy and Indian show going on later this morning in town, that he was out for a ride with his horse. He also had a travois on the back, a V-shaped wooden frame of two poles, lashed together over the back end of the horse and netted behind to carry things. As he came closer, I waved to him, but he didn't even notice me. Even when I moved out of the way, he didn't look at me. He just kept slowly riding by. Then I saw what he was carrying in the travois.

There was a boy, about ten years old, riding on it, in authentic Native American dress. The boy didn't look too good. I also noticed the blood dripping down the side of his face, and a large cut across the forehead. Being a doctor, I instinctively turned and walked toward the boy.

"Are you alright?" I asked, staring at the boy.

The boy looked white, like all the blood had drained from his body.

"Kid. Hey, Kid. Do you need some help?"

The boy continued to ignore me, staring beyond me as if I wasn't there. I was worried that the boy might be dead.

"Sir!" I yelled up at the rider on the horse. Still no response. Frustrated, I ran up to the rider and poked at his leg. That's when things got real exciting.

The man finally turned to me, not with a look of confusion or bewilderment, or even panic or concern about the sickly child he was carrying. He looked angry. I could have handled him just being angry; it was the flying tomahawk I didn't like.

"What the—" was all I could say as he whacked at my face with the tomahawk. I narrowly missed getting my head split open.

Thinking this guy was a total nutcase, I stepped back, ready to run. That was a good move on my part, for the man turned his horse and travois around and charged at me.

I started running. I ran for a few seconds, then realized Kirby was gone. I looked for him as I continued to run, all the while the crazy horse-riding tomahawk flailing freak was coming after me. Needless to say, no matter how fit I was for running, I wasn't going to outrun a horse. I had to think fast.

Diving off the path, the Indian galloped past me. I looked back as he rode by, and that's when I found out where Kirby was. He was in the arms of the little Indian boy on the travois. Now I wasn't sure what the boy would do to Kirby, but I had heard of Indians using dogs for food. I couldn't let that happen to my Kirby.

The man turned around on his horse and headed back for me, the whole time yelling, "Yee-yee-yee-yee!" Not sure what it meant, but with the tomahawk flying, it probably meant I was dead meat.

As much as I loved Kirby, I certainly didn't want to be scalped trying to rescue him. But I figured I might have a chance to get him if I dodged out of the way, then turned back for Kirby while the lunatic guy switched around.

That plan would have worked great, except that I slipped when I tried diving out of the way. Thankfully, I didn't end up with a tomahawk going right through my head. But I did get a nice gash just above my ear as I hit a large rock near the side of the trail. That wasn't the worst of it. While I lay bleeding from my head wound, the crazy guy hopped off his horse and came running at me with his tomahawk and yelling, "Yee-yee-yee-yee!" His eyes really scared me. They were dark red, almost glowing in the morning light. I closed my eyes and turned away, not wanting to look any longer.

I was sure I would be dead in a few seconds, or at least scalped and left bleeding to death. Apparently he was not too keen to strangers asking for help. I guess that maybe he's a bit overly protective of the boy in the travois. Who knows? As I lay there with my eyes closed, waiting to be scalped, I noticed he had stopped running. I opened my eyes to see him looking behind me, farther up the trail. That's when I heard the train. My first thought was that a nearby train was moving along, somewhere a few miles away. But this sounded like it was coming right at me from down the trail. That would have been fine if there were train tracks, but there were none. There hadn't been any for a few decades. Apparently, somebody forgot to tell the train that piece of information.

Just to add to the bizarre events, the Indian that was ready to scalp me, turned and ran away. Although he didn't go far, or at least he didn't have to. He suddenly faded away as he ran into the woods. The horse, travois, little boy—everything disappeared too. Except the train. It was merrily chugging along right at Kirby, who was lying on the trail, shivering and scared.

Whooo! Whooo! Chugga-Chugga Chugga-Chugga Whooo! Whooo!

I didn't have much time to react. The train barreled down on me as I tried desperately to pull Kirby away. But the train went right through us. A cold chill ran through us as well, the coldest I had ever felt, even living in Minnesota all my life.

It was over in a matter of seconds, but the chill still stayed for hours. I grabbed Kirby and ran back down the trail to the parking lot where my car was. Every few seconds I would turn back, thinking I heard a train, or the galloping of a horse. Even now when I'm walking outdoors on a trail, I listen, hoping that I don't hear the sounds of ghostly hoofs, the whizzing of a tomahawk as it flies by my ear, or the whistling of a train barreling down on me from nowhere.

History:

The Root River Trail system stretches for miles, connecting several towns along the way such as Lanesboro, Rushford, Houston, Fountain, and Harmony. One hundred years ago, the trail was a busy railroad, transporting people and goods all across Southeastern Minnesota and beyond. As the railroad industry dried up, and the automobiles took over, the railroad beds were slowly converted to paved biking and walking paths.

One local resident claims to have heard a train while jogging on the path in the early morning hours. It could be that he simply heard the train from a distant track still in operation. Still, I did find it interesting that there was a train accident years ago. In 1916, major flooding on the north branch of the Root River caused a railroad bridge to drop four feet as a train crossed. Although I could not find out how many people were injured or died in the accident, it could be a basis for why there is a ghostly train inhabiting the early morning Root River Trail system.

Prior to the railroad coming through, the trail was used by Native Americans. They had spent centuries using the Root River waterway and trail, traveling from the Mississippi River to the Black Hills in South Dakota. The Oneota, and later Dakota, Iowa, and Winnebago tribes used the trail in annual migrations from their sprawling summer villages, to winter hunting grounds on the western plains. Knowing that it was a major transportation route for the Native Americans, there could very well be some truth to the hauntings described above.

Local residents of the area have reported seeing ghostly figures walking along the trail in a westward direction. Visitors and tourists have also seen them, usually in the early morning hours just around sunrise. Most sightings are of two adults and several children, dressed in traditional Native American clothing. They are typically traveling with several dogs and a loaded travois.

The ghost-like figures do not stay long; once approached they quickly disappear into the trees, or vanish into the nearby fields. It's as if they want to be left a lone, to continue their journey westward to the Black Hills.

Native Americans that live nearby indicate that the ghostly figures are their ancestors. They are returning to this world for a brief time, to live once again along the Root River Trail and journey from the river valley to the prairie lands of the west. One wonders if, in the fall, we see the ghosts traveling west, then in the spring, they must be traveling east, coming back from the Black Hills. So, the next time you take a walk on the Root River Trail, keep an eye out for any wandering Native American Spirits, and an ear perked for a train whistle.

Field Trip:

I've been biking on the Root River Trail many times, and have enjoyed it immensely. It's a fantastic place to go bike riding. I encourage anyone to do so. But perhaps waiting until mid-morning or later is best, if you're afraid of ghosts. The early morning trek on the trail can seem a little spooky, with the wet dew on the grass along the side of the trail, and the trees hanging over the top of you gently blowing in the wind. It can be very quiet on the trail in the early morning hours, and with the wind blowing through the trees, it sometimes sounds like the whispering of voices.

I stopped out at the Root River Trail one morning, starting in Lanesboro. From there I went south a few miles, absorbing the beautiful fall morning weather. With my trusty Digital Audio Recorder of Really Eerie Noises (D.A.R.R.E.N) at my side, I was ready for any ghosts lurking in the woods.

Unfortunately, with it being a bit windy, my digital recorder didn't pick anything up except wind. Even when the wind died down, I found no EVP recordings. I took a few pictures, and nothing unusual showed there either. I guess the spirits had the morning off.

I wasn't expecting much to appear. Personally, I feel it's difficult to capture paranormal activity on a long bike trail—unless you have an exact location as to where frequent incidents occur. In the research I performed, I found no evidence of a particular location along the Root River Trail that was haunted. I went with Lanesboro, based on it being one of the oldest towns along the trail and rich with history.

Even though I found no evidence, perhaps you will on your next visit to the Root River Trail. Bring your bikes, plenty of water, and a digital recorder or two. Who knows, maybe you too will find yourself running from a Indian spirit or dashing out of the way of a ghostly locomotive train. Keep an eye on your dog, too.

Chapter 21

Hotel Clara

"As I fumbled through my thirty keys while standing in the stairwell, I heard this hideous scream."

Location: Red Wing

I never believed in the supernatural until I started working at the St. James Hotel in Red Wing. Sure, I'd read ghost stories and have watched lots of ghost movies. I've even had a few friends that swear they'd seen a ghost. But I figured it was some mental problem they had. But now I know. Ghosts are real.

It was almost surreal during my first few days at the hotel. I was very excited to be working in the magnificent building, housing over sixty rooms and was built back in the mid 1800s. It would definitely be a fantastic place to work. That is except for the ghosts.

I felt better about working there once I befriended the maintenance man who sympathized with me. He knew how much I hated being there by myself late at night. "Terri, you need help locking up?" he'd say while checking up on me around midnight. He knew, based on other employee's stories, that that's when things would start to happen.

The first incident was pretty mild compared to the other stuff that happened later. I was working late, as usual, trying to finish some paperwork. After several bottles of Coke, I had to make a pit stop in the ladies room. It was more of a closet than a bathroom, three feet wide and about eight feet long. The toilet was on the one side, a cast iron sink was in the middle, and a closet full of hanging clothes was on the other end.

Like I said, the ghostly experience was mild; it was just some light tapping on the wall of the bathroom while I was busy using

St. James Hotel in Red Wing,
where many recent paranormal
activities have been reported.

it. Normally I wouldn't have thought anything of it. "Just a minute!" I yelled, thinking it was one of the housekeepers, or perhaps the maintenance man. It could have even been one of the other managers, coming back to do some late night work. Nobody else would be in this section of the hotel; it was off limits to guests and most employees.

The tapping on the wall continued, three taps in a row, separated by a brief moment of silence. Finally, I couldn't take it any longer. I finished up and hopped outside, expecting to yell at someone. But there was nobody there.

The experience could have been written off as just someone walking by and tapping on the wall. But I knew that wasn't the case. The floors creaked. Really bad. If anyone had come into the area I would have heard the creaking floorboards in the 150-year-old part of the hotel. There was no sound other than the tapping. Plus, the door into the area was locked, so very few people would have access to this back area.

Not thinking much of it, I finished turning the lights off in the area and headed out through the locked door. At the last second, I realized I had forgotten my keys. That's hard to do, because I have about thirty of them for the hotel. There's not much I could do about it; with such a large building there tends to be lots of keys for the different areas. But it's also hard to forget them, being that combined they must weigh a couple pounds. I went back into my office and flipped on the lights. I gasped, startled at what I saw.

I saw my keys neatly placed on a shelf, too perfect for any human to arrange. Each key on the ring was lined up next to the other in an exact symmetrical pattern. I've tried several times since then to do that with my keys, but I can't. It was as if someone or something was holding onto them, keeping them aligned in a perfect position. What was even weirder was that the keys were on a shelf over in the corner of my office, a spot difficult to get to because of the way the furniture was configured. I knew I didn't put them there. There was no way I could have. And when I reached out to grab the keys, I felt a cold chill run through my hand, up into my body. At that moment I decided I had enough, and quickly headed out of the hotel.

The other incident that happened a few months ago was terrifying. It was around midnight again, and I had just finished with some work up in the kitchen. I came down the elevator and went to my office area. To get to it from the main hotel, you have to go through a stairwell area on the second floor. I went through the first steel door just fine, leaving the main hotel. As I fumbled through my thirty keys while standing in the stairwell, I heard this hideous scream. It's difficult to explain how it sounded, but it nearly gave me a heart attack. The scream was something like a cross between a sick cat and a wailing wild child. It only yelled once, but that was enough for me.

I turned to look at where the sound was coming from. It was down in the corner of the stairwell, on the floor right behind me. The stairs were dimly lit, so it was hard to see what it was that made that sound. I knew something was there, but instead of waiting around for the ghostly thing to jump at me, I frantically searched for the key to my office area. Finally finding it, I went in, all the while talking to the ghost, telling it to go away, and that I was here to help the hotel.

Still terrified from the demonic scream, I immediate left work, with my body trembling all the way home. I was beginning to realize there was definitely some paranormal activity going on at the hotel. It's one thing for someone to explain ghosts, but it's something entirely different to live through the experience. I kept hoping I would not find any other ghostly activity. Unfortunately that was not the case.

Thinking (and hoping) the paranormal events were in the past, I continued working at the hotel. I tried hard to ignore the strange events, to put them out of my consciousness. Yet deep down, I could feel something paranormal was going on in the hotel. And a few weeks later I came face to face with it, a dark shadowy figure in the stairwell.

I was walking through the stairwell area as I do countless times during the day. But this time, late at night of course, I opened the door to see a dark shadow from behind the door. My first thought was to quickly close the door. But that would leave me stuck in the office area. The only way out was through the stairwell. I trudged through, passing by the dark shadowy figure, not wanting to look back at it. Coldness filtered through my body as I sensed it moving toward me. I felt as if it came at me, running right through my body. A cold bone-chilling feeling spread through me as I rushed down the stairs out to my car. I was done working late at night after that incident. I'd only be there if someone else was with me, or at least nearby.

There have been countless reports of activity at the St. James hotel by numerous individuals, both employees and guests. It probably didn't help that the hotel was built on a Native American Burial ground. With several employees and guests dying in the hotel over the years, I'm guessing there's a few restless spirits wandering the hallways at night. The place is definitely haunted.

History:

The St. James Hotel is loaded with history. Built in 1875, funded by eleven local businessmen, the hotel was an impressive building right from the beginning. With its three floors of over sixty rooms, it was a lively place to say the least.

After about thirty years, Charles Lillyblad eventually bought the hotel, and the Lillyblads remained owning it until 1977 when it was bought by the Red Wing Hotel Corporation. Shortly after buying the hotel, Charles fell in love with a waitress working there named Clara, and soon they were married. Together they ran the hotel until 1931 when Charles died. Clara continued running the place until her death in 1972. Of course, according to some employees and guests, Charles and Clara are still running the place—in a more haunting way than before.

Honestly, there are too many paranormal incidents to report. I'm thinking the hotel may deserve its own book about the activity here (I kept thinking about the Stephen King novel, *The Shining,* as I toured the hotel). I've put in a few of the notable incidents and history of the place in the paragraphs below.

After an excellent lunch at the Veranda, a local restaurant in the hotel, I visited with a couple employees to get the inside scoop on what has been happening. I noticed immediately how serious both were about the hauntings that have been going on. Both had firsthand experiences with the paranormal activity.

First, there's the incident with the tapping on the wall when going to the bathroom. One of the employees was trying to use the bathroom, but somebody was knocking on the wall outside. She had checked outside immediately after the tapping sound, but nobody was there. She also misplaced her keys, and found them neatly arranged in an odd part of her office room. From that day forward, she knew something odd was going on at the hotel. But when she was visited by the strange howling creature in the stairwell, she knew for sure the place was haunted.

As described in the story above, a small creature of some sort bothered her one night in the stairwell area going from the hotel to her office area. She couldn't see what the shadowy figure looked like, but really didn't want to either. It howled and shrieked at her, sending a terrible chill deep into her body. She tries not to go through the area late at night anymore, although that is the only way to her office area.

The employee across the hall from her has had an eerie incident as well. During the first few days of work, strange notes were given to her. They were written in a childlike handwriting, and said things like, 'Who are you?' then later, 'I know who you are'. Since the employee had confidential human resource information, her office was locked up and nobody except her was allowed in. That made the mystery of the handwritten notes even more interesting. She was one of only a few who had a key to her office.

Historically, there may be several reasons the place is haunted. First and foremost, the hotel was supposedly built on top of Native American burial grounds. They had discovered this during the digging of the hotel's foundation, which makes me wonder why they continued building it. Perhaps the spirits are still quite disturbed after all these years, trying to scare everyone away and in turn receive some peace.

Several guests have died in the hotel over the years due to unknown causes. Employees would enter the room only to find somebody dead in bed, apparently dying of a cardiac arrest. Other times they have been found in a chair, dead from the same reason. Perhaps they were visited in the middle of the night by a ghastly apparition, scaring them to death where they lay. Nobody is really sure, the deaths remain a mystery.

Employees have died in the hotel as well, with no clue as to why. One engineer in particular died down in the back room of the basement. Recently, an employee has had the door to the room pushed shut on its own. This has happened several times to them, making them feel as though an invisible force is trying to lock them in.

Years ago, a night clerk was found dead one morning by the milkman. He had been badly bruised and beaten. The assumption was that he had been mugged sometime during the night. But by who? A person or a ghost?

Mr. Lillyblad himself had a tragic ending. Rumor has it he killed himself, jumping off a nearby bridge, plunging down into the Mississippi River. Nobody is really sure why this happened, and nobody wants to talk about it. Perhaps the evil spirits within the walls of the hotel made him do it.

There's a room down in the basement where an old well was located, used back in the late 1800s. Apparently a girl had been accidentally locked in the room and eventually drowned. To this day, employees hear the voice of a girl in the basement, coming from the old well room saying, 'Gonna let me out? Are you gonna let me out of here?' Just recently the stained glass door to the old well room has developed a crack, as if somebody has been kicking at the door from inside. There's also been reports of a knocking sound coming from within the room.

Another interesting aspect of the basement is that several rooms have been closed off, cemented over, and are no longer accessible. Could this have been done to prevent people from visiting rooms containing evil spirits? It makes one wonder what may still be in those closed up rooms, and what may come out if they were someday opened up.

It has been reported that Clara haunts the third floor of the hotel, wandering from room to room in the middle of the night. She was a very busy lady in life, perhaps she is trying to remain busy in death, always floating around to check on things to be taken care of. Charles also haunts the building, roaming through the hallways of the second floor. Not as busy as Clara, but still moving among the rooms and checking on things.

Housekeepers have had ghostly encounters as well. They've been cleaning rooms and have seen someone move in a nearby room or hallway. But when they go to see who it is, nobody is there. Several times this has happened, with no explanation available.

Chefs working in the basement have looked out into the bar area, only to find faces hovering, staring back at them into the kitchen area. But the faces have no bodies, and when looked at long enough they slowly vanish. Perhaps the spirits are hungry.

People have heard children giggling and playing down in the basement with the lights off, even when they know nobody is down there.

Some guests have left in the middle of the night, spooked out by their shutters flapping up and down on their own. One guest in particular tried to ignore the paranormal activity, but eventually got scared as the blinds on the windows began moving up and down rapidly. He left his room and complained to the front desk that the place is too haunted to sleep in.

As you can tell, there are many reports of paranormal activity here, with a lot of history that most likely qualifies the building as one of the most haunted places in Minnesota.

Field Trip:

This place by far was one of the creepiest locations I have ever seen. At any moment you felt like something was going to jump out at you. And this was during the middle of the day. Countless times I questioned whether I wanted to be doing this field trip. I imagine a full paranormal investigation late at night would be quite the ordeal. I'm not sure if I would be a part of it, but I think for the sake of science and understanding, a complete investigation is needed. Especially since it appears as though one has never been done.

For now, I was okay with using my digital audio recorder and taking a few pictures. I first checked out the bathroom where the tapping incident occurred. I couldn't find any evidence to either prove or disprove the activity. I originally thought that banging pipes would provide an answer. But the walls were solid, and I couldn't tell if there were any pipes inside. And if it were anyone playing a joke on the employee, it couldn't have happened. The floors creak terribly in the area. Anyone trying to sneak in would have been heard twenty feet away.

Pictures and recordings didn't reveal anything in the office area. At first I thought I had a picture of a full apparition, sprouting up along a nearby wall. But then I quickly realized it was a reflection off a nearby mirror. You always have to be careful with mirrors and shiny objects, they can easily look like ectoplasm, orbs, or even apparitions in the picture.

Next we (two managers and myself) toured the second floor, where Charles supposedly visits occasionally. We checked out one room (the showroom). It had a radio playing on an end table, which the manager indicated was not normal for a showroom. Perhaps a ghost turned it on, hoping to listen to a good song or two.

After walking out of the showroom, we walked by room 213 where somebody apparently had died. On the digital recorder I did pick up some possible EVPs. The voice sounded like a male, with a low gruff voice. I listened many times, and after cleaning the audio up with some computer software, I still couldn't tell what the voice was saying. It would be interesting to find out what sort of voice Mr. Lillyblad had. Perhaps he had a gruff voice.

We then went up to the third floor where Clara is supposed to haunt. Right when it was mentioned "Clara's floor", I got an EVP of a whispering female voice. It sounds like the voice is saying, "everybody can loose" then later, "sometimes have a drink". It's really hard to figure out what the voice is saying, but there's definitely something being said.

On the fourth floor we visited with a few housekeepers for a moment. When they found out I was here about the ghosts, you could tell they sort of stiffened up, as if they didn't want to talk about it too much. One of the housekeepers had some paranormal experiences in the hotel recently. While talking to the housekeepers, I walked around, mentally asking if Charles was there. I immediately got an EVP response that sounds like, "the man's not here". Which I suppose could be true, if Clara were responding, thinking Charles had died.

Several other possible EVPs were captured, but it's not clear as to what they are saying. It's also hard to verify them as EVPs, being that I was taking a walking tour and was talking during it. We would also occasionally bump into other people along the way.

In the basement we turned the lights on and were immediately startled by a table that had been moved out of place. For unknown reasons, a small table by the elevator had been pushed out into the middle of the hallway. There was no logical explanation as to why it was moved, and you could clearly see that it was originally supposed to be by the elevator wall, based on the leg imprints in the carpet.

We checked out the back room where the engineer died, but I did not find anything unusual there—although I personally felt spooked, with the hair on my neck standing up several times. And when I was in the old well room, I definitely felt something. It was sort of a sad and depressing feeling. Keep in mind, I'm no psychic medium, but I could tell it didn't feel happy in there. Even spookier were the red rust stains where the old well had been filled in with cement. It almost looked like dried blood.

Needless to say, overall I felt like the place was haunted. I think having a paranormal investigation overnight at the hotel would produce some interesting results. But perhaps you can do your own mini-investigation. Have a bite to eat down in the basement some night. Just keep your eyes and ears focused on the old well room in the corner. And if you hear a girl's voice saying 'gonna let me out?', be careful. You never know what type of spirit you might be letting out.

Chapter 22

Houseman

"One word came from her lips, gurgling as she said it. Houseman."

Location: Rochester

'll never forget as a young boy looking into that old woman's creepy eyes. Pale and cloudy eyes, staring like a zombie at me—more like beyond me—with her mouth open in a silent scream from within the dark rickety elevator. And that word that crackled from her mouth, "Houseman". My hair still stands on end when I hear the word…

Mom had an appointment at the Mayo Clinic down in Rochester. Since we lived several hours away in St. Cloud, and Dad was off on a business trip, she informed my younger brother and I that we would be coming as well. It would be an overnight trip, staying across the street at the Kahler Hotel. I remember thinking about how great the hotel adventure would be for my brother and I; both of us needed a break from the boredom of middle school.

We arrived at the hotel just before noon, and after parking the car, we headed for the hotel lobby. My brother and I ran around in the hallway, anxious to explore the old hotel. After several near collisions with other patrons, Mom interrupted our fun.

"Quit running around!" she said in a half whisper, trying to be polite and not yell down the hallway.

Why did she always yell at me? No matter how hard I tried, my younger brother never got in trouble. I suppose that goes with the territory of be a big brother.

The lobby was quite elaborate, ornately detailed with classic fluted pillars, red satin draperies, and dark, highly polished

Kahler Hotel in downtown
Rochester, where a ghost is reported
to ride the elevators and visit people
in the tunnels underneath.

oak doors and trim. The desk clerk sparkled in his shiny pin-striped suit, further signifying that this was a first class hotel. The clerk continuously smiled at my mom while she asked about early check-in. With a polite nod and a few scrambles to verify records, the check-in process was complete and we were on our way to the room.

I could tell this place would be fun, especially with the elevator buttons revealing twelve floors to explore. Mom pushed the third floor button while my younger brother and I jumped, making our initial ascent in the elevator shake, but also producing a look on my mother's face as if she thought the cable might snap. She threw a stern glance at us, putting a halt to our devilish jumps.

She ran her hand above the panel of buttons, stopping at the top to point out where the pool was located. That alarmed both of us, perplexed as to how a pool could be at the top of a building. Thoughts of water, swimmers, and beach balls crashing down through eleven floors while we slept kept us focused for the remainder of the ride. I didn't realize it at the time, but the ride up felt sad and depressing. Thinking back, I'm sure the morbid feeling I had was because of the ghostly old woman.

Once we unloaded the suitcases in our room on the third floor (after a ride to the twelfth floor and back—by a unanimous request of both my brother and I), we started our exploration. Hotel adventures were rare for us, which made the experience that much more intense. With Mom busy with her checkups, David and I tore out of the room on our own and ran to the staircase. Nowadays parents would never leave their children unattended and let them roam around in a strange building all day. But years ago, it seemed normal. Go figure. I know I wouldn't leave my kids only for more than a minute.

The door to the staircase from our third-floor hallway was large, at least four times as wide as us, making it heavy and difficult to open. We pushed hard, finally opening it to a brief rush of stale air, smelling foul and rancid, like dead bloated fish washed up on a shoreline.

Shrugging off the smell, we hopped our way down the wide staircase, counting steps and listening to our echoes before finally reaching the first floor. We opened the door and walked into the main lobby area. People rushed past, staring into the distance and not noticing us at all. We felt like ghosts among the people, who themselves seemed like zombies wandering aimlessly around the place. We zigzagged through the zombie crowd, eventually arriving at the other side of the lobby.

On the wall were various pictures framed and covered with glass; photographs of famous people past and present who had visited the hotel—Bill Cosby, Admiral Byrd, Eisenhower, Ronald Reagan, Helen Keller, and my personal favorite, Joe DiMaggio. For a brief instance, an old woman's face flashed in the reflection of the glass. I stepped back, shocked at the appearance.

"Did you see that?" I asked my brother while pointing to the glass.

"Yeah, there's a bunch of pictures of old people on the wall."

I shook my head. "No, not them, the old lady. I saw her reflection. Kind of creepy."

"Helen Keller?" said my brother as he looked closer at her picture.

My brother obviously didn't see the old woman's face. It wouldn't be the last time I'd see her face.

We spent the next hour wandering back and forth through the main lobby, up to the balcony, then back down again, dreaming of what it was like to be famous, parading through with news reporters and gawking fans asking for autographs. Or what it would have been like to be a Secret Service Agent, guarding the President of the United States while he smiled and waved to the crowds on his way to his room.

My brother noticed some stairs to the far end of the building, just beyond the restaurant. The staircase brought us into an amazing labyrinth of tunnels that we followed for at least an hour. We got lost several times, but with some keen reading of the maps located on the walls, and a little luck, we found our way back to the hotel. At one point I freaked out, turning a corner in the tunnel and running right into that same old lady. Except I didn't bump into her—*I went right through her.* I dropped to the ground, gasping for air and shivering.

My brother stared at me and said, "What did ya do that for?"

"I just—did you see—" I could tell my brother didn't have clue what just happened to me.

With my recent spooky incident, I was done running through the tunnels. We eventually found our way back to the hotel and waited for an elevator ride up to our room. Dozens of people were waiting as well, so we decided to check out the elevators on the other side of the building. With a short run we arrived at the other elevator. Nobody was waiting to get on, which seemed odd since it was such a busy place. My brother pushed the button and the door immediately opened, revealing a small cherry-wood-lined elevator with a miniature crystal chandelier dimly lighting the area. We hopped in and pushed the third floor button.

To our astonishment, the door quickly closed and we began a rapid ascent not to the third floor, but all the way up to the eleventh floor, which was for private patrons only. We thought that was cool, thinking again about the presidents and royalty that most likely stayed on the private floor. Perhaps we would get a glimpse of someone important when the door opened.

Instead of royalty, we were treated by a chilling rush of air, similar to what was in the staircase area earlier. Along with the frigid wind came a slim, nicely dressed elderly lady with a very pale looking face. She paid no attention to us at first as she casually turned around to face the door and waited for the elevator to start moving.

Then it clicked. I recognized the face. It was the same lady I saw in the reflection of the glass at the main lobby. And the same lady I walked through in the tunnels. As if reading my mind, she turned around and stared at me. It was a blank, morbid look, heavy with sadness and depression. One word came from her lips, gurgling as she said it. "Houseman". At that moment, the elevator began a speedy descent, bringing a brief instance of weightlessness to my brother and I. The ghostly old lady stared at me and repeated, "Houseman".

"Awesome!" was all my brother said. He apparently didn't think anything of the lady saying *houseman*.

I said nothing and only gulped hard at the fear lodged in my throat. The lady came closer to me, inches from my face and repeated a third time, "Houseman". I backed up against the elevator wall, shaking not from the shifting elevator as it made its swift drop, but from my knees as they trembled with terror.

The elevator slowed to a halt as the old lady turned back to the door, all zombie and stiff like, and walked right through it. I dropped to the ground, dizzy from the fear that engulfed me.

"What's up with you?" my brother said as he shook my shoulder. "You look like a ghost."

I looked at him and could tell he still had no clue what had just happened. "Did—did you see her? She walked right through the door!"

"See who?"

"That spooky old lady that came in here from the eleventh floor. She walked right through the door."

Helping me up, my brother shook his head and said, "You're crazy. I think you've had one too many Slushies."

The rest of the afternoon and evening came and went without incident. Most of the fun came from watching several hours of cartoons and then doing mega belly flops on the beds. We liked to perform the flops with our door wide open, to encourage audience participation.

When Mom arrived to the room we were allowed to go swimming; we didn't spend much time there due to us thinking that at any moment the swimming pool would come crashing down on the rest of the hotel—with us in it. We also stayed clear of the elevator with the spooky old woman.

Eventually I fell asleep, but woke up several times in the night from loud thuds outside the room. My mom and brother were not bothered by the sounds, so I ignored them and went back to sleep. I didn't sleep well, with nightmares of the old lady floating around the room or waking up to find her hovering at the foot of my bed. Morning finally came and I asked Mom if we could check out early. I didn't want to spend another minute in the hotel, for fear of bumping into the ghostly old lady again.

I'll never forget my stay at that hotel, and in my several visits since then I've had no haunting incidents. But every time I step into an elevator, any elevator, I think about the creepy old woman and her chilling stare. Sometimes I find the elevator I ride in gets cold—cold enough to see your breath. That's when I close my eyes—the last thing I want is for a ghostly apparition to float through the door and spook me, saying some strange word like, "Houseman".

History:

The tale told above represents a reoccurring theme at the Kahler Hotel. Several individuals that have stayed there have mentioned an old lady riding the elevator, or the feeling that someone is in the elevator with you, even though it's empty. Some attribute the incident of the ghostly lady to be the late Helen Brach, known as the 'candy lady', who mysteriously disappeared after leaving the Kahler Hotel back in February 1977.

She had just finished with her checkup at the Mayo Clinic, and was scheduled to fly back to Chicago where she lived. For unknown reasons, it appears as though she never flew back. Rumors indicated her butler (she called him the houseman) picked her up at the hotel. The last person to have claimed talking with her was a clerk at a gift shop in one of the tunnels underneath the Kahler (connecting it to the Mayo Clinic). The clerk indicated Helen Brach was in a hurry, and that her houseman was there to pick her up.

Thirty years later, the body of Helen Brach has yet to be recovered (although she was declared legally dead in 1984). Some investigators believe she was abducted somewhere near the Kahler Hotel by organized crime thugs from Chicago. Why? Apparently, it may deal with bad horse trading. Helen Brach loved horses and liked buying them, but a few deals seemed too shady for her; she believed a couple high-priced horses were actually worthless.

Upon finding out, she was planning on going to the authorities, and with her twenty million dollars worth, she was going to make sure they caught the thugs. As it turns out, it is speculated that the thugs got to her first. They supposedly took her from the Kahler Hotel and disposed of her body in one of the many steel mills in Gary, Indiana.

Could the old lady haunting the Kahler Hotel be Helen Brach? Is her spirit desperately lost, riding the elevator up and down in an attempt to find her way home? It's hard to tell, being that there are thousands of guests visiting the hotel, most of which are there to visit the Mayo Clinic. Perhaps some patients, spiritually speaking, never leave.

Occasionally, there are patients for the clinic that have serious, terminal illnesses. This can be depressing for them, with some choosing that suicide is better than a long and painful death. With this in mind, their stay at a hotel in Rochester may be their last. There have been many reports in Rochester over the decades of suicides either in hotels or shortly after checking out. This could be why a few guests staying at the Kahler have reported feeling overwhelmingly sad and depressed. Perhaps they were visited by a few sad and depressed restless spirits.

Field Trip:

With the stories of ghostly sadness and haunting old ladies, I decided to check things out for myself. The Kahler Hotel is located downtown Rochester, Minnesota just off Center Street and Second Avenue. With twelve floors (the twelfth floor is the pool), I meandered through each floor, audio recorder in hand, looking for anything ghostly.

As far as the sad, depressing sensation in the hotel, I only experienced that on the third floor, along with a slight heavy feeling on the fourth. Not that it means those floors are haunted, but after analyzing the audio file (using Audacity software program), I noticed a few zaps and clicks that I did not recall hearing while I walked. In particular, the light near the elevator was flickering, and the audiotape at that moment recorded heavy interference. Of course, anyone with a bit of electrical knowledge would tell you that a flickering light can cause a static charge, or zapping sound. Still, it was interesting that it all happened at once, near the elevator.

There was also electrical interference showing up at most of the doorways in the stairwells. But a loud, interesting popping noise happened on the seventh floor. I can't explain what it was, but it didn't sound like normal electrical interference. Could it have been the ghostly sound of a gun firing as someone ended their life? Could be.

On the tenth floor, I passed a cleaning lady talking in a foreign language to some other guy, who responded in the foreign language. Seconds after that, with nobody near me, the audio recording clearly picks up an elderly lady saying something like 'Arthur?' I found that to be very eerie. I don't recall seeing any old ladies outside their door while I walked by, let alone asking for anyone named Arthur. Perhaps it was Helen Brach, stating the name of her murderer.

The last interesting event was when I left the tenth floor via the stairway. An old woman opened the door before me, heading into the hallway. She was short, with short white hair, and wore large, thick round glasses. Her clothes were casual, with knit pants and a tie-die shirt. What spooked me out was her gaze—she walked right by me, staring blankly into the distance as if I wasn't even there. Kind of ghostly if you ask me.

What made things even more interesting was that a minute later, after I went down the elevator to the lobby, I saw her sitting in the front entrance area. She was still staring blankly out the door to the hotel. Was she a ghost? Did she follow me down in the elevator? Perhaps it was just a guest waiting for her test results from the clinic.

In conclusion, I found some interesting feelings of sadness on the third and fourth floor, a strange voice on the tenth floor, as well as an old lady that walked by me with an eerie look. Nothing to write home about, there were no ghosts flying all around. And I didn't find anything unusual in the elevators, except the occasional electrical interference. Is the Kahler Hotel haunted? I'm not sure, but why not stay overnight and find out yourself.

Incidentally, I checked out the Plummer Building at the Mayo Clinic. It's an old, gothic-style building built in the 1920s, complete with gargoyles at the top, looking down on all those who pass by. I found nothing unusual in the building—no ghosts or ghouls, or any sadness or depression.

Lastly, there are countless tunnels underneath Rochester, connecting all of the Mayo Clinic buildings together, as well as some hotels and shops. I used to do computer consulting for Mayo back in the late 1980s, and had the opportunity to use the tunnels. Most of them were well lit, allowing you to comfortably walk from one building to the next underground. But some tunnels were downright creepy. Some had little to no lighting available, but these were not for patients; they were for staff only. I was told there were more tunnels, not accessible to even employees that connected other parts of the city. I wondered what lurked down in these off limit tunnels—monsters? More ghosts? Who knows? I was just glad to get out of the tunnels and back up above ground.

Chapter 23
Room with a Deadly View

"The ghost woman began screaming, a piercing shrill that made my hair stand on end."

Location: Wabasha

I wished they would have told us about Sarah before we booked our room. If we would have known beforehand that the hotel was haunted, well, I don't think we would have stayed there. Especially in room 25, where all the activity occurred. If you like ghosts, it's a great place to stay. I don't, so will probably never be back there again, at least not long enough to hear the moaning of Sarah as she looks for her lost husband…

My husband surprised me and picked the place to stay. We love taking a few weekends out of the year to sightsee some of the tourist traps around Minnesota. Since we lived in downtown St. Paul, it was nice to venture out into the smaller towns around the state and briefly experience life from that perspective.

I was usually the one choosing the place to go, but this time my husband mentioned he would like to see the eagles in Wabasha. He was excited enough that he booked the room himself.

"This place is incredible, Gayle!" he said as he looked online at the hotel. "Anderson House. That's the place to stay. It's not too far from the Eagle Center."

I could tell his mind was made up. For him, that meant it was really important. He usually did not have a preference on much of anything. I quickly said, "That's wonderful, dear. Let's book it." I wasn't going to take any chances. The last vacation he charted out ended up in disaster, as he forgot to book the room. We ended up staying in a sleazy motel out in the middle of nowhere. That was scary enough, but not like the spookiness of ghosts and goblins.

"Jimmy will love the eagles," my husband said. Jimmy was our oldest boy. "And Jeffery will love the lunch buffet at the hotel." Our younger son Jeffrey loved mealtime. He hoped one day to be a chef, perhaps thinking that he would be able to eat food all day and get paid for it.

"I don't want to stay at somebody's house," said Jeffrey as we pulled into the Anderson House parking area. He was not at all happy about the trip, wanting instead to stay home and play video games like your typical teenager.

"The Anderson House is not a house, it's a hotel," I replied.

"Built back in the 1850s," added my husband. He was very excited to stay in the hotel. From the looks of it, probably more thrilled with the hotel than with visiting the Eagle Center.

After parking the car and unloading our luggage, we checked in and headed to our room. It was room 25, the Governor's Suite. Even though it was one of the more expensive rooms, the extra room was well worth it. We opened the door to the room and found it to be quite large, with a king bed at one end and a nice sitting area on the other.

"Awesome room!" said Jimmy.

My husband quickly corrected Jimmy and said, "This is the room for Mom and I. You guys are staying in room 24."

Jimmy grabbed the keys for their room and waved Jeffrey over. The two boys quickly checked out the room and after only a minute came back.

Jeffrey said, "We like this room better. Can we stay here?"

Jeffrey gave us a puppy dog look, the kind that made you melt and give in to whatever he wanted. I looked at my husband; I could tell he didn't want to switch.

"Sure. That's fine with us," I said, although my husband was not at all pleased with the decision. He gave me that 'why the heck did you do that' look, then rolled his eyes. After

The Anderson House in Wabasha,
where it is said to be haunted by
several ghosts late at night.

fifteen years of marriage, I had gotten used to it. Of course, if I would have listened to him, the kids wouldn't have been so scared.

After my husband and I got our suitcases unpacked and we settled down into our rooms, Jeffrey burst into our room. "Mom! Dad!" The look on his face made me jump. He was all pale and his eyes looked big and scared.

"What's wrong?" I asked, rushing to hold him.

"It's Jimmy. He came running into our room all freaked out."

"Where is he now?" my husband asked.

"He's underneath the covers of the bed and he won't come out."

We went over to room 25 to investigate what had happened. Sure enough, Jimmy was scrunched up in a ball underneath the covers, shaking.

My husband came over and flipped the blankets back, exposing a frightened and whimpering Jimmy. "What's wrong?" my husband said, forcing a smile on his face. I could tell even he was worried. "You look like you've seen a ghost."

All Jimmy could do was nod his head. That made my husband's smile disappear for a moment. "Ghosts, huh? Well, there's no such thing as ghosts."

Jimmy shook his head this time and pointed out in the hallway. All of us instinctively turned to look, expecting to see some ghoulish figure floating in the doorway. Nothing was there of course, but we all felt a little spooked out.

I went over to Jimmy and hugged him. "It's alright, Jimmy. I'm sure you just saw a reflection in the mirror, or something like that.

Jimmy sat up in bed, more relaxed now that we were there, and said, "No I didn't! They were real!"

"Two ghosts?" said my husband with a chuckle. He didn't believe in ghosts.

"It's not funny!" responded Jimmy. "There was a man and a woman coming up the stairs at me. One had a funny top hat on. The lady had a big wide dress. I thought they were from some old costume show, but when they reached the top of the stairs— " Jimmy couldn't continue. He was too scared.

"He told me they disappeared into thin air," added Jeffrey.

Although everyone was a bit nervous with Jimmy's 'ghost' incident, we still wanted to see the National Eagle Center down the street. It was a fascinating visit, getting to see live American Eagles and learn about all the history on them. Nothing strange happened while we were there, but the walk back to the Anderson House was disturbing to say the least.

"What's that light over there?" asked Jeffrey. All of us turned to where he was pointing, out over the river. A small blue light had formed just in front of the Anderson House along the shoreline. It hovered in place a moment, then floated out over the water. It continued slowly across the water until it disappeared into the trees on the other side of the river. That's when we heard the scream.

"What was that?" I asked, looking toward the Anderson House.

"I'm not sure," said my husband, who began walking briskly to where the scream had come from. "But it sounded like someone was in trouble. You three stay here."

My husband ran to the side of the Anderson House. We could see him stop and stare at the ground. After a moment, he came back to where we were.

"Well, what was it?" I asked.

"Odd. There's nothing there now. But when I walked up and looked, I could have sworn there was a women's body on the ground. Like—like it had fallen from above. From a window."

I could see that the boys were very alarmed at what their dad was saying. To diffuse the event I said, "Let's head in and have a treat."

We decided to get some ice cream cones from the restaurant and head up to our rooms. Relaxing and playing a few games of Scrabble might take our minds off the recent disturbing events. Unfortunately, when we opened up the door to room 25, we saw the window wide open, with the wind blowing the curtains into the room. My husband leaned out of the window, then back in with a confused look on his face. "This window is right above where I thought that lady was."

Needless to say, the Scrabble game didn't go that well. In fact, Jimmy kept coming up with strange disturbing words like, 'scream', 'dead', and 'horror'. Several times while playing the game, the window would fly open, sending a chilling blast of cold air at us. My husband even tried locking the window, but it would still open on its own. After several games of Scrabble, we decided an early bedtime would be good for us, especially since we wanted to get up early and watch more eagles. But sleeping was not an option that night.

"Mom! Dad!" I heard from outside our door. It was Jimmy and Jeffrey, both pounding frantically on the door. "Let us in!"

My husband jumped out of bed and ran to the door. The boys dropped into the room, then got up and ran to our bed.

"She's there! She's there!" cried Jimmy. As he hugged me, I could tell he was bitterly cold.

"Who's there?" I asked.

Jeffrey replied, "That lady Dad saw. She's in our room, standing at the window."

"I think she's going to jump!" said Jimmy.

That was all my husband needed to hear. He raced over to room 25. After a moment of silence he said, "Honey, come over here."

I came over to the room, with the boys following closely behind, not wanting to be left alone. To my amazement, the boys were telling the truth. There, in front of the open window, was a woman with her hands to her face as if in distress. It certainly didn't look like any ghost. This woman seemed real. At least until I tried to comfort her.

I reached forward to her shoulder, but my hand went right through. That part of my hand went numb, sending a deep chilling sensation into the rest of my body. I jumped back, terrified of the incident. "Ahhh!" I screamed. The boys screamed as well. Even my husband screamed. The woman didn't notice us and just kept staring out the window, looking far out across the river.

I calmed down enough to ask my husband, "What do we do?"

"Well, if it is a ghost, I don't want it here. We need to tell it to go."

"Go where?" asked Jimmy from behind me.

"I don't know," replied my husband.

"Anywhere but here," said Jeffrey. "I don't want to be here either."

My husband mustered up enough courage to yell at the ghost. "Go away!" He waved his hands at the ghostly woman, but it did nothing but continue to stare out the window. My husband walked in between the ghost and the window. That's when things started happening.

The ghost woman began screaming, a piercing shrill that made my hair stand on end. Then the ghost walked toward the window, going through Richard. Richard later explained it was as if someone had pushed a large bag of ice cubes through him. It nearly stopped his heart from beating.

Once the ghostly woman reached the window, she jumped. Richard turned to try and grab her, even though it would have made no difference being that it was in fact a ghost. He looked down and saw the woman lying on the ground below for a moment. Then it disappeared altogether.

After a brief moment of silence, my husband said, "Come on, let's get out of here."

I didn't disagree, which was unusual for me. The boys were happy to leave as well. We packed up our things and drove home. We've returned to Wabasha many times since the incident, but we'll never stay at the Anderson House again. Don't get me wrong, it's a great place to stay—if you like ghosts.

History:

This tragic story is based on the haunting of a young woman named Sarah from back in the early 1900s. She was deeply in love with a man, meeting with him many times in the area. The Anderson House was one of their favorite places to meet.

After a few months of dating, they met one night at the Anderson House. Sarah did not realize it at the time, but the man was preparing to leave, heading down the Mississippi River by boat and never to return. She was devastated with the thought of him leaving. The man had no choice but to leave. Sarah, apparently heartbroken over the loss of her lover, killed herself by jumping out the third-floor window of the Anderson House.

A different version of the story indicates that Sarah was in fact meeting with a married man. One night he came to the Anderson House and told her of his existing marriage, and that their affair would have to end. She threatened to throw herself out the window if he left. Sadly, he left, and shortly thereafter, she jumped to her death.

Tracking down information on suicides that occurred decades ago is virtually impossible. Those types of deaths were not typically recorded. At most, you would find them listed simply as dying accidentally. In the research that I did, I could not find any information about anyone named Sarah, or anyone jumping from a window (except from what was told in the stories). Still, several paranormal investigator groups have visited the Anderson House, and have found some interesting activity.

One such group had a camera flash continually go off, all by itself, until the batteries were dead. The individual with the camera promptly left after that event, obviously spooked out by it. At one other time, three members participating in the investigation jumped, startled as their cell phones simultaneously went off. It was not clear who had called them, but if it were someone from the spirit world, I'm sure it would have been an interesting conversation.

Ghostly figure staring out a second-floor window at the Anderson House. Other pictures taken seconds before and after show nothing but curtains.

Some guests staying at the Anderson House have reported seeing people they believed to be ghosts. They were usually dressed up in clothing from the late 1800s or early 1900s. At one point, guests were confused to see a man and a woman walking up the stairs, with the man wearing a top hat. The woman was wearing a Victorian period wide-skirt dress. Once the couple reached the top of the stairs, they disappeared.

Other guests have found a man up on the third floor wandering aimlessly around in the hallway. Upon seeing you, he would come up to you and ask for your ticket, as if you were riding a train, or possibly a ferryboat across the river. This particular incident is the most alarming in my opinion. It's one thing to have ghosts simply reenacting a part of their own past, not paying any attention to you. But when they interact with you, that's scary. Who knows what else they may do to you besides take your ticket.

At any given moment, you might find yourself hearing voices. Eyewitnesses have indicated they've been touched or brushed by an unknown entity while walking through the main floor restaurant area, and sometimes in the upper level hallways. The ghosts will also whisper your name in your ear. But when you turn there to look, nobody is around.

The other known activity has to do with all the cats running around the Anderson House. Cats have become a landmark for the place, with large statues of them out front and around the town of Wabasha. What's interesting is that, occasionally, a cat will go berserk. They will run around crazily or jump continuously at a wall. They will also stare and hiss at the corner of a room, as if they see some ghostly figure hovering there.

Chapter 24

Silent Movie Ghost

"What alarmed me more was the eerie face bobbing up and down above the stage."

Paramount Theater in Austin, where it's reported to be haunted by the ghost, possibly the previous owner from the early 1900s.

Location: Austin

The owner of the bar told me about the spooky things that might happen when working late at night. What he didn't tell me was how terrifying it was to meet a ghost, especially one who was angry at loud music.

I was very excited to get the job as night manager for the restaurant and bar in Austin. With my new degree in restaurant management, I was eager to prove my theories. What made it even more interesting was that the place I was hired at used to be an old theater, the old Paramount Theater. It was amazing how they changed things, taking out all the theater chairs and leveling off the floor. In my opinion, I think that's what made the ghost angry. It seemed like he wanted it the old way, back when it was a theater running plays and movies.

"Good luck closing tonight, Terri," said the owner of the bar. He smiled and added, "And watch out for George. Remember, he doesn't like the loud music."

I didn't like how they named the ghost. It was bad enough to worry about bumping into something strange when walking around a corner, but to have a name for it? Not for me, especially when the old theater-turned-bar building was so old, over sixty years old. It also didn't help that tonight was Halloween.

Tonight was the big Halloween dance with live music from a local band. Every year it was always fun. Loud too. Very loud. Which made me nervous, wondering if 'George' the ghost would come out. It didn't take that long for me to find out.

"I thought I told you to keep the marquee sign outside off until dark?" asked the owner.

"It was off," I said as I walked out to look at the sign. I quickly realized it was now on. "I didn't turn it on."

"Well, then who did? That sign costs a lot of money to run and we don't need it on during the day."

I smiled and said, "George must have done it."

The owner was not amused, even if it was probably the truth. I walked over and shut if off again, only to hear it flip back on while we walked away. That spooked me. It also told me that tonight would probably be a lively one. I really didn't believe in ghosts, but it was hard to ignore the fact that I couldn't come up with any logical reason the lights turned on by themselves. Cautiously, I walked back to the switch and flipped it off, not wanting to stay there too long. That's when a cold chill went through my body, like I was dunked in a bathtub full of ice cubes.

The next few hours were uneventful, other than a few power glitches due to the gigantic speakers the band was using. I couldn't attribute that to any ghost, but I also didn't completely rule it out. The band played into the evening with its loud rock and roll. I was all for that. The louder the better for me. I just wish George the ghost felt the same way.

Several times during the band's performance, the volume would drop unexpectedly. The soundman working the volume controls was freaked out at one point when he watched the controls move on their own. I couldn't explain how the controls were moving, but I wasn't that concerned about it. What alarmed me more was the eerie face bobbing up and down high above the stage.

"Great music," I said to the lead singer of the band while they were on break. "I like all the classic rock tunes."

He nodded as he chugged a glass of water.

"But I'm not sure about the song where you wore those masks. The guy you had up in the balcony was too creepy. Several people were very upset. And I thought I told you nobody is allowed up in the balconies?"

The singer stared at me, confused. Finally he said, "Man, we didn't have anybody up there."

I turned white when he said that as I remembered how ghastly the face looked, and how angry it looked. If it was a ghost, I didn't like the idea of it being around. I spent the next few hours being spooked at everything that moved. At one point, I screamed at someone wearing a mask coming out of the men's bathroom. Of course that scared them too, and they ended up leaving. The owner of the bar wasn't too happy about that.

Closing time finally arrived, and it looked as though I was going to make it through my first day of work without any major incidents. Sure, I had a drunk or two that needed a cab, and a scuffle outside in the street that the police had to break up, but there were no more ghosts. That is until I was left alone to lock up.

I had just been up in the rear balcony area turning off lights and locking up the liquor. As I began shutting off lights,

I could hear a strange noise coming from down below on the main floor. As I walked down the stairs, I could tell the sound was coming from the bar. It was the mixers. Both mixers were running by themselves. I quickly walked over to shut them off, but could still hear one running, in the distance. I then realized it was the blenders upstairs in the balcony bar. Of course, when I went up to turn them off, the mixers down below were back on.

I can't say that the mixer incident was that scary, but it certainly was weird. Especially when I walked over to turn them off. A dark, depressing sensation hit me, followed by a freezing gust of cold air. That was strange in and of itself, as there were no doors are windows open. I would have been fine if the night ended on having only spooky mixers, but then I heard footsteps.

I looked ahead to the stage where the band had played. The footsteps were definitely coming from the stage, but nobody was there.

"Who's there?" I asked. The footsteps stopped. I peered into the darkness of the stage, but still could see nothing. The footsteps started again. They sounded like they were getting louder, as if something was coming closer. The bar area I was in was a good fifty feet away from the stage, but I could tell there was nobody wandering around on stage.

"Who's there?" I repeated, and again the footsteps stopped. That's when I started to hear the screeching sound, and that's when I started to get scared.

"Whoever you are, you're not supposed to be here. Get out of here before I call the police." I still couldn't see very well up on the stage, so I grabbed a flashlight from the bar and flipped it on. I shined the flashlight over at the stage back and forth, looking for the source of the squeaking and the footsteps. I would have been happy to find someone standing there, but I didn't find anyone. All I found was a swivel chair from the bar, rotating around and around, *all by itself.*

That's when I got really scared, and the hair on my arms and neck stood straight up. I also started to feel dizzy, like I had drunk too much Halloween rum punch. But I hadn't a drop of liquor all night. Then there was that feeling. It felt like someone was watching me from somewhere in the room. I began moving my flashlight back and forth through the bar area and stage, but found nobody. Just then, the swiveling chair stopped and I heard footsteps running away.

When the footsteps stopped, I had this strange notion that whatever was watching me was now up high. Not in the rear balcony bar area, but up above the stage. I didn't want to look up there, for fear of seeing that ghastly mask. But I had to do it, almost as if something was forcing me to shine my flashlight there. That's when I saw it.

The ghost had this grotesquely looking white face, all droopy-like and angry looking. I couldn't tell what the rest of it looked like, other than some sort of round gray mass. I was too petrified to scream, especially after it noticed I saw it. That's when it floated off the side balcony right at me.

I didn't need to be told what to do next. I ran. And I didn't look back. I ran out the front of the old theater-turned-bar and down the street. I didn't stop running until six blocks later when I ran into a convenience store to call the owner. He thought the whole incident was a joke and told me to go back and lock up properly. I told him to go do it himself and that I quit. There's no way I would ever set foot back in that bar.

Years later, the bar was turned back into a movie theater. Some friends of mine went to a movie there and asked me to come along. I said no. The last thing I wanted was to end up sitting in the theater and have George the ghost fly down at me from the movie screen. No thanks. I'll stick to watching DVDs in the comfort of my ghostless home.

History:

There was an original theater, the Park Theater built in 1919 on the existing theater location. Sadly, a tornado had come through and destroyed it. Interestingly enough, the projectionist from the theater had just left at the time of the tornado's arrival, to go over to the theater across the street. By the time he came back out, he watched as the tornado pulled apart the Park Theater.

Years later in 1929, the Paramount Theater was built over the foundation of the old Park Theater. Movies and plays were performed there until 1975, when it was closed. In 1977, the theater opened up as a bar, with the floor leveled off in the main area and up in the balcony. That's when most of the paranormal activity occurred.

During a Christmas party dance, one individual taking pictures ended up capturing what is thought to be a ghost. He had taken a picture of a Christmas tree in the upper balcony above the stage to the left. Floating around part of the tree was this white, transparent, murky entity.

Another incident occurred during a dance (yes, it's a constant theme that the ghost does not like loud music). The band was on stage, playing loud rock and roll throughout the night. At one point, the band always puts on some crazy masks for a particular song.

The eerie part was that the audience saw someone way up high above the stage, poking their head through the bars near the rafters and wearing a really spooky-looking mask. The band members were complemented on their music, but were told that the guy high up in the balcony area with the spooky mask was not appropriate. He was much too scary. The only problem was that the band members did not have anyone up there. Furthermore, it's not at all easy for anyone to climb up into the location where they saw the ghost.

One night, while a bar manager was closing up, she heard footsteps coming from the stage area. She was concerned, knowing nobody else should have been there. When she looked up at the bar, the footsteps stopped and a swivel chair started turning all on its own.

Many times blenders at the bar would go on all by themselves late at night. Bartenders would turn them off, only to find them running again on their own a little later.

Granddaughters of a projectionist who used to work in the theater stopped by a year or two ago, excited to see the old place. They took some pictures of the theater, and interestingly enough, a round object appears up on the ceiling in one of them. The theater is an atmospheric theater, meaning it had an amazing ceiling that would glow dark blue, and tiny lights would twinkle like stars. It's an amazing site. There are only four theaters like it left in Minnesota. What was surprising was that it appeared as though a moon was in the picture. There is no lighting system setup to display a moon. Furthermore, the granddaughter used no flash. I personally looked at the photograph and could not disprove it in anyway, other than if someone perhaps digitally enhanced it. But it would be difficult to manipulate the picture digitally, being that it was from a camera with film.

Lighting can be an issue in the theater as well. It was a common occurrence to have the Marquee lights out front turn on by themselves. The manager would lock up for the night, shutting off the dozens of bulbs out front on the Marquee light. It was important to shut them off late at night, as they were expensive to run. Needless to say, the manager had gotten in trouble many times when the ghost turned them back on at night and the owner would arrive in the morning to see them all lit up.

The soundboard has had some activity recently. An employee was working around the theater area, listening to some loud music, Steely Dan's *Aja* to be exact. After a few minutes of working, he noticed that the music was turned way down. He walked over to the soundboard to find out that something had slid down the volume control. Nobody was in the theater except him. Perhaps the ghost has a poor taste in music; Steely Dan's *Aja* is an incredible CD to listen to. A classic from years ago.

The building remained a bar until 1987, at which time it closed down. But within the last few years, the Paramount Theater has reopened, becoming available for movies and plays once again.

One last bit of history on the theater. In 1945, there was a terrible electrical storm that came through the Austin area on Halloween Night. During that time, the spire out front on the theater was hit by lightning, sending the spire crashing to the ground. Just recently, they have finally repaired the spire, allowing us to now enjoy the building in full splendor. Perhaps the ghosts are finally at rest too, happy to see the place restored to its original magnificence.

Field Trip:

My field trip started with a detailed history of the Paramount Theater. It always helps to have the background, in order to understand why the place is haunted. I had firsthand information, coming from a source that grew up in the area and had worked in the building over the years. He's also experienced paranormal activity himself.

After the historical discussion, we decided to walk around, taking pictures and having the digital audio recorder running as we went. A couple of minutes into the tour, a couple of interesting things happened.

At 5:35 on my recorder, I noticed a loud screeching sound. It was really loud. I don't recall hearing anything like it while standing there talking. I can also here someone whisper 'danger' or something like that. It's hard to tell, due to the screeching sound going on. It certainly was not my voice, or the voice of the employee giving me the tour. There were only two others in the building at the time, and they were way up front in the office area.

I took a couple pictures of the main theater area while standing up on the stage. Two of the pictures ended up capturing a green phantom light or mist in the center of the seating area. I don't recall any green lights located anywhere near the theater seats. The light, however, could have come from my camera. Right before I take a picture, a tiny green L.E.D. light shoots out, I think to help me focus on the pictured I'm taking. The odd thing is, I don't think I've ever captured it in a picture. It always shuts off prior to me snapping the photo.

I also captured a couple orbs (little balls of energy) in the theater room. At least that's what they look like. As I've said, I'm not a big fan of orbs. Especially when you're taking pictures with other light sources in the room, or places that will reflect light from your flash. Dust can also cause one to think an orb is flying around. I'm pretty sure the orb was caused by strong high-powered lights hanging overhead, though.

Every few minutes I would catch some Electro-Magnetic Field (EMF) activity on my recorder, or at least that's what I believed it to be. Crackling and zapping could be heard. It could mean there's some paranormal activity, or it could be due to me walking by some electrical power lines or conduit. Still, the EMF sounds happened several times when I was in the middle of the theater, with no signs of electrical wiring. Of course, it doesn't necessarily mean there's a ghost flying around at the time. Still, I always take note of that on my recordings, as there could be the potential for ghostly activity in the vicinity. It also seems like sometimes the zapping or popping sound is a signal, letting you know a real EVP may soon be occurring, or has just happened.

At 18:35 on my second audio recording, I heard a weird sound, then some whining or moaning. It was during the conversation about the strange soundboard event where something mysteriously turned the music down. Perhaps the ghost was still letting us know he didn't like the loud music.

Another interesting bit of information has to do with the 'stairs that go nowhere' down in the basement. It's kind of weird, but there's a closet with cement steps that lead up to nothing. Upon further investigation, it turns out that they were steps from the foundation of the old theater, the one that was demolished in the tornado back in the early 1900s. When it came time to rebuild, they ended up with a new floor plan, and the cement stairs ended up in a broom closet. Still, it adds to the mystery of the building and makes you wonder if the stairs are some portal into another world.

We also walked around back in the dressing room area, and even checked out the old air conditioner, one that you could walk through. Apparently, it was one of the first air conditioners in Austin. Water would drip down in a large chamber, about the size of a small car, while a giant fan blew air through it. It was definitely a cool room (no pun intended).

Orbs and green light (highlighted in square) in theater area.

While touring the attic above the dramatic theater ceiling, I caught a strange squeaky sound, almost like a high-pitched voice. Perhaps it was an EVP of some singer from long ago, still screeching away the high notes to some forgotten top forties tune.

Another odd thing that happened was that a cell phone went off while we were talking about how the ghost does not like loud music. We joked about having a loud party some night in the theater—that's when the cell phone went off. And the ring tone for the phone was something like the song from the Exorcist movie. Of course, it wasn't a ghost that called, but it did wake me up a bit.

Probably the spookiest thing that happened was an EVP I captured while upstairs in the projector room. The employee and I were talking about the projector room, and I asked where the light switch was. Two seconds later you can clearly hear a voice say something. It was a raspy voice that seemed to say 'Art'. I'm not sure if that was a person that worked there long ago or what. Who knows? All I know is that it gave me goose bumps when I heard it during playback.

Based on my own personal experiences, the place didn't feel that incredibly creepy. But it was the middle of the afternoon. Perhaps the ghosts are currently dormant, satisfied that the old theater is no longer a loud and obnoxious bar. The spirits in the place may feel at rest for now. That's not to say they couldn't come back, or that there may be those who have had recent paranormal experiences there.

One idea on who the ghost is that haunts the place is that it could be the old owner from back in the early 1900s. Apparently he did not like it when the building changed into a bar, with alcohol and loud music being broadcast everywhere. Even today, strange things tend to happen when really loud music is played. So stop by sometime, perhaps even rent out the Paramount Theater for a loud heavy metal music party. Then watch and see who shows up. Just don't be surprised if the music keeps getting turned down mysteriously, or a ghastly apparition flies out from the rafters above.

Chapter 25
Sleeping with Buffalo Bill

"I can't get the ghostly face of Buffalo Bill out of my head."

Location: Lanesboro

'll admit it's not something you hear every day. And admitting that you slept with Buffalo Bill, well, that's kind of weird too. Not like I wanted to by any means. It just sort of happened. I rolled over in my bed and there he was, snoring away. Except this was the *ghost* of Buffalo Bill. I knew he was a ghost because this was the 1980s and William "Buffalo Bill" Cody had been dead for over fifty years. But what convinced me that it was a ghost was that I could see right through him.

I like to do a lot of biking, and Lanesboro has some of the best biking trails in the Midwest. The trails are from a set of old railroad tracks, stretching for miles across the beautiful hills and bluffs of Southeastern Minnesota. Since I was from Anoka, on the northwest side of the Twin Cities, I decided to stay at a Bed and Breakfast while in Lanesboro. It was October and the leaves along the trail were changing colors, making the trip even more spectacular. My trip would have ended on a pleasant, happy note, with thoughts of fall-colored leaves swirling by me as I peddled along the trail. But I can't get the ghostly face of Buffalo Bill out of my head.

Nothing unusual happened at first. I parked my car on the side streets of downtown Lanesboro and checked in to the Bed and Breakfast late Friday afternoon, room number one. I was excited to get going, hoping for a cool, evening ride before sunset—but after I had a quick meal. The owners of the Bed and Breakfast said I could lock my bike up out back. That worked fine for me, I never liked carrying my bike into buildings, or locking it up on the top of my car. But when I rode my bike

Mrs. B's Bed and Breakfast in Lanesboro,
where strange things have occurred,
possibly from the ghost of Buffalo Bill.

to the back of the building, I almost did a front wheelie as I stopped quickly to avoid hitting a tombstone.

My initial thought was, *Who would bury a person in their backyard?* Then I wondered if there were any others buried. I cautiously tiptoed to the bike rack further back. After locking up my bike, I looked up at the Bed and Breakfast, noticing someone staring down at me from the second-floor window. It was a man with long gray hair and mustache with a goatee. The man just kept staring out the window, not noticing me at all.

"Who's the guy upstairs with the beard and mustache?" I asked the Innkeeper when I came back inside.

She replied, "What guy? You're the only one staying tonight."

I shrugged it off, thinking that maybe I just imagined the guy. They served meatloaf and mashed potatoes for dinner. I wasn't a meatloaf kind of guy, but it tasted great. The owners sat down and ate with me too, giving me a chance to ask them about the grave in their backyard.

"That's Mr. A," replied one of the owners. Then added with a laugh, "He's our permanent guest."

"Seems kind of odd to have a grave right behind the building," I said while finishing my meatloaf.

"Actually, it's not," said the other owner. "It was quite common back in the 1800s to be buried on your own land near your home."

"Are there any more graves back there?" I asked.

One of the owners winked and replied, "Could be. I guess you better watch where you step."

I finished my meal quickly, not because I was that spooked out by the graves in the backyard, but because I wanted to get an evening bike ride in. I had studied a map of the trails already and knew which way to go. I could get in a good twenty miles of biking before it would get too dark. That was if I had a bike that was usable.

I went back to unlock my bike, only to find it vandalized. Somebody had let the air out of both my tires and bent my seat around. Worse yet, I couldn't pump the tires up. Luckily, I always carry several tubes for my bike. Within fifteen minutes, I had my tires pumped up with new tubes and was ready to go. The seat turned around was easy to fix, although I'd forgotten about that and sat down incorrectly, making me slide forward and hit the top bar on the frame. That didn't feel too good. Still, I was not going to be denied my evening bike ride, and was able to get at least ten miles in.

The trail ride was uneventful and allowed me to relax and enjoy the beautiful fall colors on the numerous trees. But I kept thinking about the graves in the backyard and the spooky man upstairs at the bed and breakfast. Something didn't feel right. I didn't believe in ghosts or other supernatural things. I figured they were just stories from crazy people who thought they saw things. I just hoped I wasn't becoming one of them. Unfortunately, that night dashed away any expectations I had of thinking I was sane.

With my bike carried into my room (wasn't going to let the bike get vandalized twice), and my eyes tired from reading a book I'd found down in the main lobby (no cable TV in the room), I decided it was time for some sleep. After a quick tooth brushing, I flipped the light off in the room and dived into bed. Within seconds I was sleeping soundly, but soon woke to a clicking sound. The light in my room had mysteriously turned on.

At first I wondered if I had forgotten to turn it off, but remembered clearly walking over to the light switch. Once again, I got up and turned the light off. No sooner had I reached the bedcovers when the light turned on by itself. I immediately looked over at the switch and thought I could see something there. *Spooky,* I muttered to myself as I went over to the switch and turned if off. I watched the switch for a moment in the darkness, trying to see if it would switch back on. It did.

That startled me, making me jump back and wonder what was going on. But what alarmed me more was that chilling sensation I got, as if some terrible, cold wind just blew through me. Still, I was tired and had no time for dealing with a malfunctioning light switch. I reached over to the lamp and unscrewed the light bulb, forcing the darkness upon me. That's something I probably shouldn't have done. Now I had no options for light, other than what little shined in from the full moon outside.

Shrugging off the light switch incident, I fell asleep once again. But the sleep was not in the least bit peaceful. I had some strange dreams—dreams like I was back in the 1800s with cowboys and Indians. Rifles were firing around me while arrows and tomahawks were flying. That's when I saw him, Buffalo Bill. Dressed in long leather boots, a leather jacket, and a wide-brimmed hat; he came running into town, shooting his pistols high into the air. He looked menacing, like he was out to kill someone. That's when he looked right at me.

I didn't need to know what he wanted. I could tell by the look on his face he wanted a gunfight. Except there was one problem, I didn't have any guns. But I don't think he cared. I started running as fast as I could, all the while his pistols kept firing at me. Just when I thought I would be filled with bullet holes from head to toe, I woke up.

Now, that would be a fine story in and of itself, but it's not the end. As I lay there in the bed with my heart pounding rapidly from the nightmare, I turned and looked beside me. I could tell something was there. The nightmare had continued. There, resting next to me was Buffalo Bill. The hair on the back of my neck stretched and tingled, making me want to scream, but I was too scared. Instead, I did the only natural thing (besides running); I tried to push him away. That, of course, woke him up. He wasn't too happy about that.

What made it even creepier was that I couldn't physically touch him. My hands went right through the body. Every time I pushed, my hands went numb, chilled by the space where his phantom body lay. After several pushes, the ghost of Buffalo Bill woke up. He turned and looked at me with his cold gray eyes.

But what surprised me the most was that he looked as scared as I did. He yelled with a deep moaning sound that prickled my spine inside and out. I screamed too (yes, I admit it), and that's when he disappeared.

One of the owners of the Bed and Breakfast came rushing to my door and pounded on it. "Are you alright?" he asked from behind the door.

It would have been easy to go over to the door and open it, telling him of the strange incident. But it was dark and I unfortunately had no light to turn on. In the process of going to the door, I tripped over my bike, bending the frame severely, not to mention my leg. Furthermore, I fell into one of the antique oak chairs, splintering it into pieces.

"Are you alright?" repeated the owner from behind the door.

I finally reached the door and opened it. At that moment, the light in my room came back on, *even with the bulb being unscrewed.* I stood there staring at the owner, not sure what to say.

"You look like you've seen a ghost," said the other owner as she looked at me from the hallway.

I laughed. I'm not sure if you would classify the laugh as hysterical. But it probably was. Regardless, I was done with the place and didn't want to spend another minute there. I grabbed my suitcase and bike and headed for the door. It's one thing to hear about ghosts, or even see things moving around. But having one in your bed? Sleeping with one? And a famous one like Buffalo Bill? That was too much for me.

History:

There's certainly a lot of history in Lanesboro. It was quite the bustling town back in the late 1800s. And Buffalo Bill was no stranger. One of the reasons William "Buffalo Bill" Cody stopped by frequently was because of his friend, Dr. Frank Powell.

Dr. Frank Powell was an Indian Scout that Buffalo Bill got to know over the years. Having a good scout back in those days was important. At some point in the mid 1850s their paths crossed and they became good friends. What's interesting is that Lanesboro is credited for being where Buffalo Bill started his Wild West shows. In fact, Mrs. B's Inn was originally the residence of a doctor, presumably Dr. Frank Powell. Upstairs is where Buffalo Bill and others supposedly planned the idea for a Wild West show. The first show took place in the building next door to the inn.

Back in Buffalo Bill's day, Mrs. B's Inn was a funeral home and furniture store, for over one hundred years. It was built in 1873, and I suppose the two businesses worked well together, with the furniture store making coffins for the funeral home.

Supposedly, Buffalo Bill visited Mrs. B's Inn often (back when it was the residence of Dr. Frank Powell's), and Buffalo Bill most likely slept there too. The current owners have not heard of any stories where the ghost of Buffalo Bill sleeps with their guests. But based on the history of the place, it is entirely possible. They say ghosts tend to haunt the places they like most. That might explain why Buffalo Bill haunts Lanesboro and Mrs. B's Inn. It's a great place to be!

According to the current owners of Mrs. B's Inn, there are some strange things going on. For one thing, the lights in the main hallway upstairs burn out at an unusual rate. At one point, they replaced all of the light bulbs, but within a few days, all of them mysteriously burnt out. They had traced the electrical wiring back to the fuse box and found no shorts or hot spots. The wires were old, but perfectly normal.

Another lighting problem occurs in Room One. Some phantom ghost appears to need the light on all the time. When the owners would leave for Rochester for the weekend, they would come back and always find the light on in Room One. Even on short trips they've come back to find the light back on. At one point, they had the light off during the day while doing some cleaning in the room. Flip! The light went on all by itself. Needless to say, the owner (who was well away from the light switch) got spooked.

The kitchen may be haunted as well. The owners have heard strange noises come from it when nobody was in there. A kitchen is notorious for having plates and pans shift on their own, due to improper stacking. But in this case, the sounds were more like things moving around, like a nearby trashcan being shoved across the room.

There's also a giant wasp nest located high in the attic. That by itself isn't so creepy, but apparently the shape is in an elongated pattern, stretched out to make it look as if it were a body. Perhaps it is a body, with a wasps nest built around it. That would certainly explain the eerie things going on.

What's more creepy than sleeping in an old funeral parlor? How about finding human bones in your backyard. Yep. The owners of Mrs. B's Inn have found bone fragments while cleaning up in the backyard area. And old mason jars too. Makes you wonder what was kept in the jars.

There is in fact a tombstone buried in the back of the inn. Although it's hard to say whether there's someone actually buried there. It could just be left over from the funeral parlor days. Apparently, other tombstones have been found further away from the building, down on the bank of the Root River. Perhaps there are people buried there, ones who could not pay their funeral bill, eh?

Field Trip:

I stopped in one afternoon to chat with the current owners of Mrs. B's Inn. They graciously allowed me to check out the place, taking pictures and doing some digital recording. Upon walking into the place, you immediately feel like you've stepped back into the past. It's a warm, cozy environment, inviting you to stay and relax.

After a few minutes discussing the history of the building, we decided to take a tour. Most of the activity had occurred upstairs in Room One and Room Three. Armed with D.A.R.R.E.N

Tombstone behind Mrs. B's Bed and Breakfast, with rhubarb growing quite well around it.

(Digital Audio Recorder of Really Eerie Noises) and my digital camera, I entered the rooms.

Room One felt perfectly normal. Granted, this was during the afternoon in broad daylight. Perhaps the ghosts were sleeping? At any rate, I inspected the room along with the phantom light switch, but found nothing out of the ordinary. In later investigation of the audio recordings, I did not find any noticeable EVPs. Although a couple of times it appeared as though some unusual sounds had occurred, but it could have been from me carrying the device around the room in my hand.

In Room Three I did feel something. Before I started all this ghost hunting, I never really thought about why I would occasionally get goose bumps, or why the hair on the back of my neck would stand up and tingle, giving you that scalp-shrinking affect. That was the feeling I got when I walked into the room. I also had an odd sensation that something was in there with us, some invisible force watching us as we walked around. It was a very creepy feeling indeed, very similar to how I felt in the basement of the Mantorville Opera House. Unfortunately, nothing showed up on the audio recordings. The digital pictures came up void of any apparitions or orbs as well. What did seem interesting was that the light was on in the room when we walked in. The owners looked at each other, smiling. There was no one else staying there that day and they had not turned the light on.

In the kitchen area, where things have been heard moving around, I had a couple photographs that at first looked like phantom figures materializing out of nothing. But after further review, it was just reflections from my camera flash on the stainless steel cookware. You always have to watch out for shiny objects. It's always a good idea to be a little skeptical, to try to disprove the possible hauntings.

Next we toured the basement. One of my favorite (not!) places. Especially knowing there were lots of dead people in it. Really. The basement is where the people were embalmed when the building was a funeral parlor. I walked into the room where the work was supposedly done, visualizing a large table in the center with body on it, and other bodies waiting their turns nearby. If there were any ghosts in the building, you'd think they would be in the room I was in. Of course, now it was just a storage area and workshop. Didn't matter what was in the room. It felt creepy.

Being a ghost hunter wanna-be, I asked to shut off the lights and go silent for a minute or two, to try and take a few pictures of some ghosts, and hopefully record a couple freakish voices. As soon as the lights were off, it quickly felt very gloomy. The hair jumped right up on my neck as I tried taking some pictures. I did not like it in there. Needless to say, I didn't quite last more than a minute. Sadly, nothing came out on the pictures I took, or the audio recording. Although I think you can hear me breathing a little heavier in the dark. Spooky indeed.

The only interesting EVP happened when I was talking about how you may not really get much ghost activity at funeral home, being that the place only had dead bodies and was not a location of catastrophic events. That once you're dead, you're dead. Right after saying that, a faint sound is heard, something like a voice. It sounded like it said, "It's not true." Although the word 'true' is clipped off. Were the spirits trying to communicate with me? I wondered if they were floating invisibly in the room, shaking their heads and rolling their eyes at me that I could be so skeptical.

The rest of the audio recordings turned up nothing. Pictures too. Based on my personal experience in Room Three and the old embalming room, it felt like the place had the potential for paranormal activity. More believable to me were the owners' testimonies. Their description of the lights turning on and off is a classic paranormal event. I sometimes wonder if because of the electricity going through the light switch, that it is an easy (and obvious) thing for the spirit to move, an easy way for them to get your attention. Either way, there's no doubt that odd things are happening at Mrs. B's Inn.

But you don't need me to tell you. Just call them up and stay overnight. Ask for Room Three, or Room One. And if they're all booked up, maybe they'll let you camp out behind the building next to the tombstone. Or perhaps stay in the old embalming room down in the basement. Just don't sleep on the table. They'd rather not wake up in the morning and find out you've been embalmed.

Chapter 26
Now Do You Believe?

"Deep into that darkness peering,
long I stood there wondering, fearing,
Doubting, dreaming dreams
no mortals ever dared to dream before;"
                    —Edgar Allan Poe from *"The Raven"*

ou can't have a Minnesota book without a Sven and Ole joke, so here it goes:

This happened about a month ago a few miles north from Rochester in the town of Zumbrota. It may sound a bit like an Alfred Hitchcock tale, but it's real. Very real.

A hitchhiker was on the side of the road, Highway 60 East of Zumbrota, late one night in the middle of a dark and treacherous thunderstorm. With his thumb jabbed out toward the road, he hoped somebody would quickly stop and give him a ride. Nobody would. To make things worse, it was raining really hard, making it virtually impossible to see more than a few feet in front of him. Suddenly, a car came from behind as he walked, slowly rolling forward like a ghost car in the rain. It continued to slow down, creeping toward him before finally stopping.

Without thinking, and wanting to get out of the rain, he instinctively jumped in the passenger side of the car and closed the door. Only then did he realize that nobody else was in the car, including in the driver's seat. The car wasn't even running. All he could hear was the pounding rain from outside.

The car began to creep slowly forward. The hitchhiker became terrified, but was too scared to even think about jumping out. The car continued to move, approaching a sharp curve in the road, with an overflowing creek along the side that was more like a river due to the torrential rains occurring. The hitchhiker was still too scared to get out, but he started praying and begging to the ghostly car, hoping it would not take him over the edge of the road and into the fast moving river to drown.

Just before the car hit the sharp curve, a shadowy figure appeared at the driver's window. A hand reached in, grabbing the steering wheel and turning it hard. The car turned safely around the bend. Once safe, the hand mysteriously disappeared through the window, leaving the hitchhiker alone once again.

Traumatized with fear, the hitchhiker stayed in the car, watching as a phantom hand reached in and grabbed the steering wheel, each time as the car approached another treacherous curve. The hitchhiker couldn't take it any longer. Mad with hysteria, he finally threw open the door, jumped out, and ran away in the pouring rain, ahead to the next town. He would never forget his ghostly car and phantom hand on Highway 60.

Drenched from the rains, he finally made it into Zumbro Falls. With his voice shaking, he ordered a couple shots of whiskey and told the bartender about his spooky experience.

Once finished, the bartender stared at him in silence, with the hair on his neck and arms standing straight up. He could tell the hitchhiker was serious.

Around an hour later, two guys came into the same bar, totally drenched and exhausted. They each ordered a couple Schells beers and sat there a moment, breathing heavy while chugging down their refreshing liquids. Finally, one of them looks over and sees the hitchhiker, then jabs his friend and says, "Look, Ole. Ders dat idiot dat rode in our car when we wuz pushin it in da rain."

I've been trying hard to figure out how to end this book. It's been a blast writing, I'll say that much. There have been some very interesting stories I've discovered along the way, and some even more interesting ghosts. Traveling from town to town in Southeastern Minnesota has brought me many different experiences. But there's one central theme across it all; people seeing ghosts.

No matter where I investigated, or who I interviewed with, they all had similar experiences. For unknown reasons they've been exposed to some unnatural events. You can call them ghosts, spirits, demons, aliens, or whatever. The fact is, a few people across Southeastern Minnesota have run into something strange and unusual. It's no different anywhere else in Minnesota, or for that matter the entire world. Countless people claim to have been visited by something they can't explain logically. Whether it's fabricated only within their minds, or physically hovering in front of them makes no difference in my opinion.

But why hasn't everyone experienced these odd events? Why is it only certain individuals are confronted with the paranormal? It makes you wonder if some people are like a magnet for spiritual activity, like a beacon in the darkness. And they may be totally unaware of it until they are presented with the right situation; living in the right place at the right time. Or in their case, I'm sure it's more about being in the wrong place at the wrong time. Either way, something gets triggered and ghosts come out. I believe to have experienced it firsthand during the writing of this book.

As I believe I've indicated, I'm one of those ghost skeptics that's on the fence. My initial plan was to work on getting an open mind about all this ghost business, trying hard to look and listen to the things going bump around me. Interestingly enough, things did start to happen.

One night after my son had taken his bath, I walked into the bathroom, only to find the tub full of water. At first I was a bit frustrated, thinking my preteen son forgot to pull the drain. I was shocked to find out from my wife that she had drained the tub, and turned the water completely off. She is not one to forget or be confused. Trust me. The only thing left for me to wonder is if some ghostly entity had stopped by, turned the water on, and put the drain plug back in.

A week later I had another experience. Every night before bedtime for my two boys, I put the empty bedtime water cups from the night before on a small ledge upstairs. Once the kids go to bed I bring the cups down into the kitchen to be washed. One night I put the cups on the ledge and walked away, only to find them mysteriously knocked on the floor. I didn't think anything of it, until I put them back on the ledge. No sooner had I turned around then they were again knocked on the floor. Nobody else was around.

Recently I've been watching a lot of the *Ghost Hunter* shows on the Sci-Fi Channel before I go to bed. I know, it's probably not the best time to be watching spooky shows, but I wanted to get a better feel for what goes on during a paranormal investigation. Especially since I would be going on one in a few weeks. While downstairs in the family room watching the TV, I began to hear footsteps out in the kitchen. I could see directly into the kitchen and knew nobody was there. I paused the show and looked into the kitchen. The whole time I could hear footsteps like something was walking around. But everybody was already up in bed.

Another time I was letting the dogs out in the backyard, late at night. I had let them out down below from the basement, with the deck up above me. While the dogs spent some time looking for the best spot to poop, I contemplated ghosts and ghouls. I also spent a moment opening my mind, almost like meditating, trying to welcome the spirits and supernatural world. Within seconds I got an answer. Something large moved up on the deck, as if a large object skidded across the boards. This can sometimes happen on a really windy day; one of the aluminum deck chairs will slowly slide from one side to the other of the deck. But that night there was no wind.

One morning at about 6 A.M., I heard some strange noise coming from down the hallway. After investigating, it turned out to be one of my son's robot toys. Of course, he was sleeping in his room, or at least trying to sleep. Nobody was around the toy, as it was resting on his shelf on the other side of his room. The next day it went of again, pretty much at the same time. That's when he came into the room, spooked. I took the toy out and put in our spare bedroom. But the next morning, a different toy came on, at about the same time. Very creepy indeed.

Like it or not, there are things happening that cannot be explained using logic and science. Perhaps we are on the verge of a new evolution in science, where ghosts and other paranormal activity are becoming more prevalent. Maybe there will soon be a day when ghosts are part of science, once we develop the correct tools and techniques to monitor them. That is, if they let us.

Which brings me to my next point. Are the ghosts playing with us? Do they have any control over their ability to manifest in our world? Sometimes I wonder if ghosts have a sense of humor. There they are, invisibly watching the ghost hunters bumping around at night in the dark, trying to capture them. Yeah, right. Something tells me it's like trying to bring down an elephant with a peashooter. Every once in a while you may irritate the elephant if you hit him in the eye, but most of the time, the elephant is the one in charge. What concerns me most is what happens if you really tick off the elephant. He steps on you. Hard. But is that the way of the ghosts? Would a ghost actually hurt you?

Perhaps to a ghost, the ultimate pain is fear, and maybe death by fear is the worst way to go. I'm not too sure about that, but I do know for a fact that a little fear of the unknown gets my blood pumping. Several times at night while I walked the dog by myself in the rural area where we live, I've pondered the thought of ghosts, angels, and demons. Are they flying about my head, watching me as I pick up dog poops? Perhaps. And who's to say they are not afraid of us?

There's an interesting thought. Do we scare the ghosts just as much as they scare us? I bet there's some truth to that. Perhaps there are things we say, do, and feel that the spirits among us hate. Or even love. There could be a level of energy coming from us that drives them into manifestation. That I could see as possibly true. Perhaps the human soul (or any soul for that matter) has an infinite amount of energy, similar to that which is contained in a single atom. With that energy, we may sometimes (without realizing it) stir up the spirits of the past, arousing them to what once was. Our own energetic spirits may spark the spirits of the past into brief fits of life.

But I digress. What I'm really interested in is if you now believe. Do you? Did any of these stories ignite the paranormal flame within you? I know many of them did for me. But can I say unequivocally there are ghosts? Maybe. But is that really what matters? Do we really need to have the perfect photo of a full-body apparition hovering above our bed? Do we need that haunting voice mysteriously captured on our digital recorder? Few would argue that, for some people, no amount of evidence would ever be enough to make them believers. For those, only their own experience with the supernatural will open their minds.

I'm guessing that for most people, the stories, investigations, and interviews contained within this book will not sway you in your beliefs one way or another. But then again that was never my real intention. I've only tried to provide a meaningful look at a few individuals around Southeastern Minnesota who have been involved with paranormal activity. All of the stories are based on real incidents, as described in the 'History' section of each chapter. The stories are real to the people that have experienced them. Very real. How would you react to waking up at night and finding a demon troll staring at you from your bedside? Or what would you do if you found yourself strolling through a cemetery and not have any idea how you got there?

Things happen. Most of the time it is explainable, wrapped up in the logic and science we have figured out over the centuries. But then there's those experiences we find it difficult to categorize into one particular science bucket or another. They just don't fit. Then what do we do? Most of us ignore them, trying hard to make it seem as if they never happened. It's only natural. Our minds tend to try to fit things neatly into piles of explainable events. When we bump into a few events that fit nowhere, we toss them out. It would be interesting to find out just how much supernatural activity is actually occurring, stuff that happens right in front of us but we choose to ignore it. Ah, that word. Choose. It's a very important word, because it leads to intention. What do you intend to see? If you believe in the paranormal, then you intend to see it, which only leads to more strange happenings. But if you choose not to believe, then your intention is to never see the things that go bump in the night.

And where do you fit in? Again I'll ask, now do you believe in ghosts? What I'm really asking for is your intentions. Do you intend to see a ghost sometime in your life? Or do you intend never to see one? The power of intention is strong, and only you can control that power. I have a feeling that those who intend on finding a ghost, will. And those who don't, won't.

There is one other aspect to all of this. You are not the only player in the search for paranormal activity. Others are involved, people who may have different intentions then you. You may want to find out more about the supernatural, even joining a paranormal investigation team. But as you hunt for ghosts, others will be with you and the overall intention will change.

I think that's what happened when I went on an investigation with Twin Cities Paranormal Society (TCPS). I went on the first night with them to the town of Mantorville, and we didn't find too much activity. I couldn't make it for the next night, and that's when they had more paranormal events. Why wasn't there more the first night? Could be many reasons. But one that I ponder has to do with me. I felt like quite the skeptic, not believing at all that a ghost would jump out in front of us. And you know what? Nothing ever did jump out. Other than the personal experience down in the basement (see the chapter on TCPS), not much happened. I felt as though I might have nullified any intentions of meeting up with the paranormal that night.

What's interesting is that I really want to find out more about the paranormal. I would like to know for sure if there is life after death, that the spirits are among us, alive and active. But I'm just not sure I want them jumping out at me when I least expect it. Perhaps there will be a day when we can meet ghosts, like going to a rock concert. The spiritual entities can float around on stage while we gawk at their magnificence. I'd much rather have that then to roll over in bed and see a ghostly shadow float across the room. No thanks.

So it seems like, for many of us, we tend to ignore the supernatural things going on around us. We choose to ignore them, not wanting them to upset our logical and structured lives. But sometimes we do not have a choice. The power of the paranormal in some cases becomes too great, for unknown reasons. You then find yourself confronted with a ghostly apparition in front of you, or coming down the steps in your house. You are not a believer (or at least were not up until then), and had no desire to meet anything from the supernatural world. Yet there you are, face to face with an apparition. What do you do? Scream I suppose. Although most people just get up and leave. Walk away from the strange event.

Others accept the unexplainable events. They find a way to explain them in their own minds. They become believers. They see ghosts. Are you one of them? Do you admit to it? What's interesting in today's society is that more and more people are claiming to have experienced some paranormal event. Years ago most feared less of the ghost and more of being locked up, sent to some State Hospital for the Insane and end up with a frontal lobotomy, or accused of being a witch and be burned at the stake. Nowadays people are somewhat more open to the existence of ghosts. After all, if you're a God-fearing man, believing in angels (and demons), then why not ghosts?

So here we are again, talking about beliefs. Is there no way around the subject? Not when it comes to dealing with the unknown. Quite honestly, there can be nothing else other than belief when talking about things of the unknown. Think about it. If it were known, then you'd have science to back you up, right? Belief would not be as critical. Whether you believe something or not is irrelevant if you can scientifically prove it. Science backs up evidence in the known world. But in the unknown world of paranormal activity, the science we have is belief itself. Which, of course, is no science at all.

You can't prove things with just your personal experience. At best you can explain the supernatural event, describing all the details of its manifestation. Yet in the end, it is only your word that can be used as evidence. Which is for the most part what this book provides. Personal experiences. That's it. But even with that, there's hope that it may have jump started your awareness of the unknown. You may be slightly more willing to turn the lights off at night, sitting in your house staring into the darkness with a camera and audio recorder. What will you find? Who knows. You and your intentions will certainly find out.

If you do find the boogeyman in your closet, don't be alarmed. After all, how many people do you know who have been killed by the boogeyman (yes, I know—if they'd been killed, you'd never know them)? And how many obituaries have you seen where the cause of death was from a ghost? If anything, death might have come from fear as the heart skips a beat while staring at the unknown. Perhaps that's a risk we all take while we dance along the line between the known and the unknown. Are you willing to dance? Which side of the line will you shuffle to?

Thankfully, not all of us need to do the fandango into the unknown. Most of us are fine sitting at home on our comfy couch watching reruns of *Gilligan's Island*. Some of us may even dare to view episodes of *Ghost Hunter*. Only a few depart on a trip through the unknown, a place where you have no idea what will happen. Thanks to a few brave paranormal investigators; they search the cemeteries and forgotten buildings of the towns we grew up in, seeing things in a different way. A supernatural way. They are willing to peer into the dark unknown places of not only our neighborhood, but also the blackness of our minds. What makes things go bump in the night? They are willing to find out. Are you?

So the next time your house creaks, and you're sitting there home alone, take a moment to ponder the unknown. Do you believe? If there's any doubt, then perhaps that's the gap the ghosts fit in, appearing out of nowhere only for a moment while you question reality. At that moment, they are there. Then gone again. Was it real? Did a ghost just appear? Already your mind is busily at work disproving the supernatural event through logic and reasoning, making it drift back to the unknown where it came from. *Ghosts are not real,* you confide in yourself. *They do not exist.* But something inside of you struggles. A part of you has seen the unknown and is forever changed. You silently wait, wanting, yet not wanting, more of the unexplainable truth that for one brief moment revealed itself to you.

Like any great mystery, the clues to the paranormal truth are sparse; only a few sleuths can put the pieces of the puzzle together and come up with the right reality. Even then, the knowledge is not easily shared. There is no great Internet in which to transfer experiences from one person to another. Or is there? Maybe that's what all of this paranormal investigation is about. Sharing the information, one event at a time. Perhaps we will eventually tip the paranormal scale, causing the floodgate of supernatural awareness to open. As thousands of paranormal investigators share their experiences, a ghostly pattern may result. Certain buildings, at certain times, in certain weather, all may add up to a probable encounter with a ghost. Which from there could lead to more measurements, more evidence, and possibly better means of capturing the paranormal events. Perhaps we will one day find ourselves believing that the paranormal is normal, and that the supernatural is natural. What then will the unknown look like?

So, grab a friend, a camera, and a tape recorder. Check out the old house you live in. Take some pictures during the witching hour in the darkness. What do you have to loose other than the comfort of your own simple reality? The worst that could happen is you find a ghost or two. At least then you can get on with your life, knowing the ghostly truth. You can finally get some sleep, knowing it's just a ghost, a demon, or poltergeist tromping around in your room, right?